Home Production of Vodkas, Infusions & Liqueurs

Stanley Marianski

Adam Marianski

Bookmagic LLC,
Seminole, Florida

Funding provided by
The Foundation for
Reading Area Community College

Home Production of Vodkas, Infusions & Liqueurs
Stanley Marianski
Adam Marianski

ISBN: 978-0-9836973-4-3
Library of Congress Control Number: 2012914825

Bookmagic, LLC.
http://www.bookmagic.com

Printed in the United States of America.

Contents

Introduction

When the idea of writing a book about vodkas and other spirits was born, I decided to leave the United States and write it in Poland. Poland has been making beer, honey wine, vodkas and all types of alcoholic infusions for centuries. This art has already been described in two classical nineteenth century books "How to Cook" by Maria Disslowa and "Universal Cookbook" by Maria Ochorowicz Monatowa. Well, I have read them both and all I can say is nineteenth century folks knew how to make alcoholic spirits very well.

For almost a year alcoholic beverages were made on a daily basis and then evaluated by our friends who at the average age of 65 years, with a lifelong experience in drinking, have become our expert panel of judges. Vodkas were made and drank even faster than opinions were stated. People there still remember how vodkas were made at the turn of the century, during the communist regime and now. Our judges would simply say: Yeah, this is what we used to drink in the past. Whether it was rowan berries, bison grass, sweet flag or other fruits or berries the judges knew it all. The streets in Poland are lined with sour cherries, walnuts, hawthorn, blackthorn, dogwood, rowan, plums, linden flowers and they are all used for making alcoholic beverages. Every time a new fruit appeared on the market we would make an infusion from it. Dry fruits like raisins, prunes or apricots were tinkered with as well.

The advantage of making spirits at home lies in the fact that a hobbyist can experiment with new fruits, herbs and spices on a whim, a luxury that commercial producers cannot afford. The factory must walk a thin line between profits and quality, for it must make money to satisfy shareholders expectations, whereas hobbyists strive to produce the best beverage possible. In time, a hobbyist becomes an artist, a professional maker of alcoholic spirits. Think of a monk who patiently grew, harvested, distilled and mixed different combinations of fruits, berries, teas, herbs and spices with alcohol. This is the art of spirit creation. A good barman can mix cocktails using ready to drink components, our vodka making artist is creating those new components. A barman might say: "what would you like to have?" and our spirit making artist could ask: "what kind of vodka would you like me to make for you today?"

During the course of writing the book we threw many drink-mixing parties which became an instant hit. We would go to a place with a bunch of bottled infusions, spice and orange skins extracts, aromatic extracts, sugar syrup and pure alcohol. We would ask: "Well, Mary what would you like to drink? Let's make a drink that you will design." As she said what she liked, we started mixing those components together and everybody would glorify the wonderful drink that Mary has just invented. Alcohol certainly brings people together.

A Different Approach to Making Alcoholic Spirits

From the start, we decided not to write another recipe book. A collection of recipes does not make a person proficient in a new skill. You have to know the How and Why of making spirits; you have to know the rules that govern the process. And first of all you have to realize that alcohol is just a tool, albeit a very important one. Once you understand how to manipulate the properties of alcohol, the rest will fall into place.

In most books the infusion is treated as the final product, a drink that has been made with spices and sugar. In this book making an infusion plays two roles; it can be made as a ready to serve drink or it can be made as a raw material that will be later used for making vodkas or liqueurs. This gives complete new meaning to the word infusion; it becomes the building block for the future. And this book provides all the rules that govern the building process; selecting alcohols of different strength, preparing common extracts such as vanilla, cinnamon or orange skins, procedures for using dry and fresh fruit, preparing sugar syrups, proper macerating times, filtering methods and much more.

By the time the book is read, the reader should be able to create his own recipe and this is exactly what we had in mind. We strive to prove that making alcoholic spirits is a form of cooking and not just mixing a few ingredients to make a cocktail. The fruit, herbs and spices are just the materials and alcohol becomes the tool. With skillful manipulation of alcohol's properties, a wide variety of wonderful spirits can be created. To get the reader started, a collection of 107 detailed recipes are included, which can be studied and used as a reference.

By carefully reading this book you will discover that producing new spirits is almost like cooking, one needs to first know the basics and then let the imagination run loose. Everything falls into its place and making new drinks becomes routine. Your spirits display constant quality, they become clear and look beautiful. At this point the process becomes an art form.

Make your drinks the way you feel they should be made, make them for your friends according to their likings and preferences. In time you will become an expert and in an instant you will spot a good recipe from a mediocre one. However, the main satisfaction comes from the fact that you can make top quality spirits from any fruit, herb or combination thereof. We don't want you to blindly follow unknown recipes, we want you to create them! Be the magician, be the master drink-maker, be the alchemist.

Stanley Marianski

Chapter 1

Alcohol and Distillation

We knew how to make wine 10,000 years ago. It was most likely discovered that when certain fruit was left unprocessed, its properties would change and the fruit would have a different taste. The discovery of alcohol was a gift from the Gods and that explanation made sense. Countries located around the Mediterranean basin were the first ones to discover the art of fermentation and they possessed the right combination of easy to ferment fruits like grapes, figs, and dates. The warm climate allowed the creation of new drinks which established a trade. While the Italians are credited with creating different types of wine by adding herbs and spices, Persia, Egypt and China were familiar with wine making as well.

Let's make something clear; we have been drinking very weak spirits for most of our history. Wine is obtained through the fermentation process where yeasts that are naturally present in fruit convert sugar to alcohol. Once the level of about 16% alcohol is obtained, the yeast die, period. Their work contributes to their demise; they are on a suicide mission; the alcohol they create kills them.

Wine was served at any occasion as it was a social drink that was taken up for pleasure. Beer was another alcoholic drink like wine dating back to the beginning of our time. The moment we knew how to harvest barley we probably discovered how to make beer. The strength of beer was usually around 4-6% alcohol by volume so it was also a weak spirit.

Herbs and spices were always of great importance in the preparation of alcoholic beverages. The main reason for adding herbs and spices to alcoholic drinks was for the benefit of their medicinal powers. Wine was considered an excellent vehicle for administering an herbal drug, since it extracted more of the active ingredients than a simple water infusion. In addition, alcohol in wine preserved the mixture from spoiling. One of the best known old digestive drinks was a cordial wine known as hippocras - the name is derived from the Greek physician Hippocrates. Its Latin name was Vinum Hippocraticum - wine of Hippocrates. It was made by inserting a mixture of spices such as cinnamon, cardamom, grains of paradise (a species in the ginger family), and long pepper, in red or white wine sweetened with sugar or honey. At this time most oriental spices were so expensive that only nobility were able to drink hippocras. One of the best known ancient hippocras was wormwood wine, a bitter tonic prepared by steeping a handful of wormwood *(Artemisia absinthium)* in red or white wine.

Hippocras was a medicinal bitter drink that was supposed to stimulate the digestive juices, expel flatulence and prevent colic. Hippocrates recommended absinthe for jaundice, anemia, rheumatism and menstrual pains. The hippocras of Medieval and Elizabethan times were rather syrupy tinctures, originally sweetened only with honey.

Man has been making tinctures for thousands of years, but the first ones were produced not for the pleasure of drinking but for medicinal purposes. Those early extracts were made with wine and herbs, occasionally with honey, and being generally bitter they did not generate much following. It took us more time to discover how to make drinks that can make us drunk faster. That discovery is known as the process of distillation.

Discovery of Distillation

The discovery of distillation is generally attributed to Arab alchemists in VIII century Spain. From then on medicinal syrups were made with stronger alcohol. The actual process, however, was kept secret until 1286, when Montpelier University professor Arnold de Villeneuve described the first distiller. He is credited with discovering this wonderful "fountain of youth"; the drink that was the answer to all problems. Even today, many agree with his theory, which may explain the quantity of spirits we drink regularly. The magic drink was known as "aqua vitae" (water of life) or "aqua ardens" (water of fire). This corresponds to the description of whiskey by American Indians who accepted the wonderful tradition of intoxication from Europeans. They simply called it "firewater."

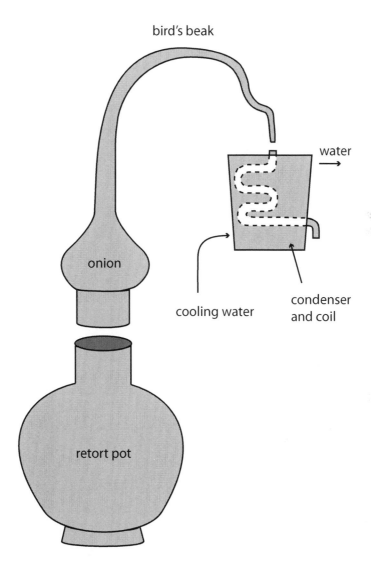

Fig. 1.1 The early Arabic distillation device that came to be known as alembic.

In 1500, German alchemist Hieronymus Braunschweig published *Liber de arte destillandi* (The Book of the Art of Distillation) the first book solely dedicated to the subject of distillation, followed in 1512 by a much expanded version. In 1651, John French published *The Art of Distillation* the first major English book on the subject.

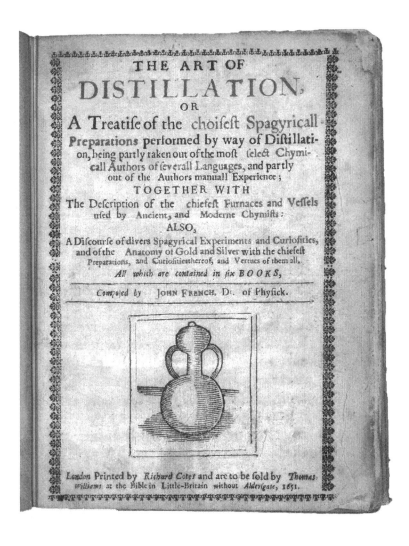

Photo 1.1 The Art of Distillation, Composed By John French, Dr. of Physick, London, 1651.

A quote from the book:

How to Make Aqua Vitae and Spirit of Wine out of Wine

Take of what wine you please. Put it into a copper still, two part of three being empty. Distill it with a worm until no more spirit comes off. Then this spirit will serve for the making of any spirits out of vegetables, but if you would have it stronger, distill it again and half will remain behind as an insipid phlegm. And if you would have it yet stronger, distill it again, for every distillation will leave behind one moity of phlegm or thereabouts. So shall you have a most pure and strong spirit of wine.

The surprising fact is that today the majority of amateur distillers use exactly the same configuration for making moonshine at home. The principles of distillation that John French described 400 years ago are still applied by many amateurs today which can be seen in the photo below. From that time on tinctures were made with stronger alcohol. Those first alcohols were distilled from fruit wines which made them expensive and beyond the reach of commoners.

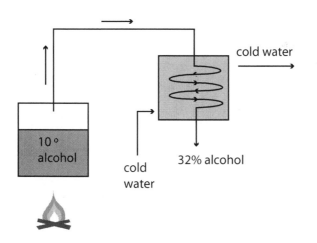

Fig. 1.2 The original distillation principle.

Photo 1.2 Home distillation using the traditional distillation process.

The traditional pot still produced alcohol of about 30% and to make a stronger spirit, the operation had to be repeated many times.

Multistage distillation using traditional pot still		
Stage	**The beginning**	**The end**
1	11% (base alcohol, for example wine)	32%
2	32%	55%
3	55%	70%
4	70%	78%
5	78%	83%

The biggest alcohol strength increase is in the first and second stages. Then it starts to slow down. To go beyond 83% will require so many stages that the operation will be impractical. Today's equipment performs multistage distillation in one single operation in a single distillation column.

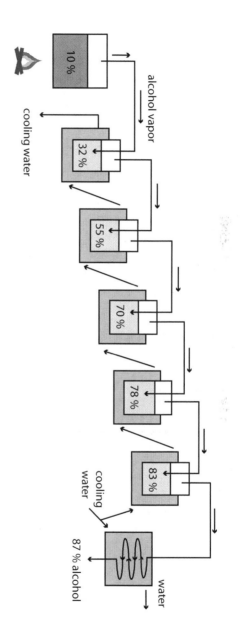

Fig. 1.3 Multistage distillation principle.

The next breakthrough occurred when we learned how to obtain sugar from sugar cane and beets. Cane plantations had mushroomed all over the Caribbean islands and Europe had fallen in love with sweet food. Expensive honey was replaced with cheaper cane sugar and we started to enjoy our herbal remedies. Once we had discovered how to obtain sugar from sugar beets which grew well in cold climates, the price of sugar plummeted lower and sugar became available to all. Alcoholic drinks became sweeter still, and we started to drink more. Then, we learned how to prepare barley, rye, wheat, rice and potatoes for making alcohols and many new types of drinks such as vodka, gin, rum and whiskey appeared.

Until XIX century alcohol was crudely distilled using the same equipment that Arnold de Villeneuve described in 1286. This produced 35% strength alcohol with poor flavor, however, the flavor was masked by adding sugar and herb extracts. In order to obtain alcohol stronger than 60%, the process had to be repeated many times which largely increased the costs of production. In 1817 Johannes Pistorius, German brewery owner, designed a modern distiller that could produce 85% alcohol in a single operation. His design had started a revolution in distilling equipment design and nowadays we can produce high quality 96.8% pure alcohol in a single operation.

Distillation Principles

Although distilling alcoholic beverages is prohibited in the USA, it is legal in many European countries and the book will not be complete if we skip the distillation process entirely. The same equipment that produces distilled alcohol can also be used to distill water or produce natural essential oils. Distillation is a controlled process and alcohols of different strengths can be produced.

Distillation equipment separates crude oil into diesel oil, kerosene, gasoline, naphtha and gas. Because all those components have different boiling temperatures, they can be separated easily by a process called fractional distillation. The same concept is employed for distilling alcohol from raw materials such as grains or potatoes. In order to produce alcohol at about 90%, a single alembic must be used so many times that the operation becomes impractical. A single distillation column will produce pure alcohol in one operation. This is almost like placing all those containers in Fig. 1.3 on top of each other inside one pipe. Such a pipe is called a fractionating column and contains a number of plates or trays which function as the containers in Fig.1.3.

1. The first step of distillation is making a fermented mash. It is made from cheap materials such as grains or potatoes. In home production sugar is commonly used for the following reasons:

- It is relatively cheap and widely available.

- Ferments fast and produces alcohol rich mash.

- It does not produce bad odors.

- It is easy to clean the equipment and discard the leftover material.

Sugar is mixed with water, fast working fermenting yeasts are added and the fermented mash is ready for distillation in a matter of days.

2. The mixture is brought to a boil and vapor is produced. This vapor consists of alcohol, water and aromatic substances.

3. The vapor enters the bottom of a long column (fractional distillation column) that is filled with trays or plates. Both terms describe the same thing. The trays have many holes or caps in them to allow the vapor to pass through. Industrial columns can be 10 meters (30') high with 1 m (40") diameter and they are equipped with 30 trays. Such distilling columns produce alcohol 24 hours a day. Smaller enterprises employ a simpler one tray design which is enough to produce a good quality brandy, gin or vodka. Regardless of the size, all fractionating columns operate on a principle called the *external reflux*. Reflux refers to the portion of the condensed liquid that returns to the upper part of the fractionating column.

4. The vapor rises in the column. There is a temperature difference across the column (hot at the bottom, cool on top). As the vapor rises through the trays in the column, it cools and becomes liquid that accumulates in the trays. The hottest vapor is in the upper part of the column and escapes to the condenser where it cools and liquefies, becoming alcohol. There is one problem: as the column gets hotter and the trays start to boil, all liquid will soon evaporate and the flow of vapor will be unobstructed. It will run up through the neck of each tray towards the condenser where it will become weak alcohol. Without boiling liquid in each tray, the column becomes just an empty pipe and we end up with a one stage alembic apparatus. The external reflux design keeps the trays always flooded with liquid alcohol. What follows is the detailed operation of the reflux column with bubble cap trays.

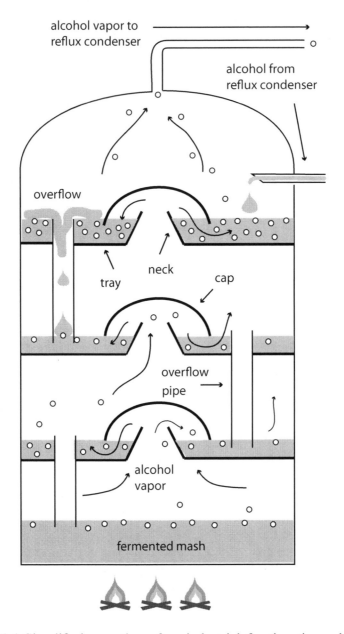

Fig. 1.4 Simplified operation of an industrial fractionating column with bubble cap plates.

A. The mash starts to boil and alcohol vapors start moving. The vapor rises through the neck of the first (lowest) plate, hits the bubble cap, condenses on its walls and becomes liquid. Some of this vapor remains in its gaseous state and heats up liquid on the first shelf increasing its temperature. As the liquid starts to heat up on the first plate it produces a vapor which now contains more alcohol and less water than the first vapor which originated from the mash.

B. This vapor rises up towards the second plate and the only way up is underneath the bubble cap. The vapor mixes with liquid on the second plate and releases some of its heat. The second plate is boiling and produces vapor which contains more alcohol and less water that the vapor before. This new vapor is rushing up towards the third (top) plate.

C. The vapor which was generated by the second shelf finds the way towards the liquid on the third (top) plate. It releases some of its heat and helps to boil the liquid. This liquid contains more alcohol and less water than the liquids on the second and the first plate. The alcohol rich vapor rushes towards the reflux condenser. There hot vapor makes contact with the cold condenser and becomes liquid alcohol.

Reflux Principle

The fractionating column can only work when the plates are holding a boiling mixture of water and alcohol. Drain the liquid away and the column becomes an empty pipe. That is why a part of freshly made alcohol is continuously redirected towards the column where it flows down on the top plate. Depending on a design and the purity of alcohol we want to obtain, the ratios vary, but about 2/3 of alcohol is re-supplied towards the column and 1/3 towards the storage. After all, the reflux alcohol is not being wasted but rather recirculated over and over again.

Commercial producers use two condensers:

- Reflux condenser
- The main condenser

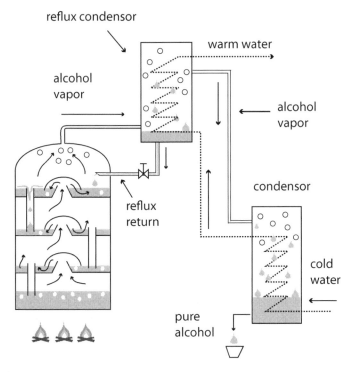

Fig. 1.5 Reflux principle.

Both condensers are cooled with water which can flow first towards the main condenser and then through the reflux condenser, or both condensers can have separate cooling systems. Operation of the reflux condenser is controlled with cooling water. Some of the alcohol vapor that enters the reflux condenser will immediately liquefy and drip down to the bottom of the condenser. From there a part of liquid alcohol is redirected to the column to keep the plates flooded. Uncondensed vapor will flow towards the main condenser where it will liquefy. This extra condenser may be considered another distillation step and another plate in the column, so obviously a two condenser design will make even purer and stronger alcohol.

5. When the level of liquid in the top tray rises too high, it overflows to the tray below. The trays must always be covered with liquid. The alcohol vapor will rush through it into a condenser and all you get is a simple alembic (Fig.1.3).

To keep trays filled with liquid a large part of distillate is redirected back from the condenser to the top tray in the column. The remaining part of distillate is taken for bottling. The downflowing reflux liquid provides cooling and condensation of upflowing vapors thereby increasing the efficacy of the distillation tower. The more reflux and/ or more trays provided, the better is the tower's separation of lower boiling materials from higher boiling materials.

There are two designs of the plates:

- Bubble cap
- Sieve plate

Bubble cap. The discussion for clarity was limited to one cap in a plate, big industrial plates of 1-2 meters in diameter carry many caps. The caps are very effective in distilling mashes which tend to be thick.

Sieve plate. Another design which is cheaper and simpler to produce is the perforated screen design which works well with thinner mashes, such as sugar or molasses. If the pressure drops, the screens will drain the liquid and the column will not work until the pressure comes back to normal which takes time. Hundreds of 2-3 mm (1/8") holes are drilled in a metal plate. The plate also has a little pan onto which goes an overflow tube. The plate must be covered with boiling liquid in the same manner as the bubble cap described earlier. The reason the liquid does not drain through the holes is due to the pressure from the vapor which enters from below. If the pressure drops too much the liquid will drain away. The holed plates are continuously supplied with reflux alcohol from the reflux condenser.

Columns fitted with plates are capable of producing a lot of alcohol and are beyond the reach of a small operator. Firstly, it is hard to believe that a person needs to produce gallons of pure alcohol every hour, secondly the pipes become 30 cm (a foot) or wider, very tall and heavy. Thirdly, to boil a huge amount of fermented mash we need boilers which are capable of generating plenty of steam. A typical house does not have enough current to operate such equipment and will have to be rewired.

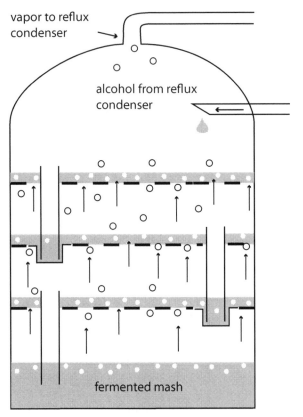

vapor to reflux
condenser

alcohol from reflux
condenser

fermented mash

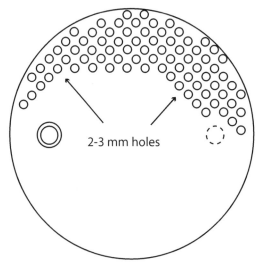

2-3 mm holes

Fig. 1.6 Perforated plate also known as sieve design.

Homemade Reflux Distilling Columns

To satisfy the needs of homeowners a scaled down version of the industrial column is offered which is capable of producing up to one liter of pure alcohol every hour. Homemade columns employ the external reflux design as well, their diameter is 1-3", two inches being the most popular, and the trays are replaced with a packing material that will allow the vapors to condense as they pass up to the condenser. This material should have as large a surface area as possible and at the same time offer little resistance to the vapor and

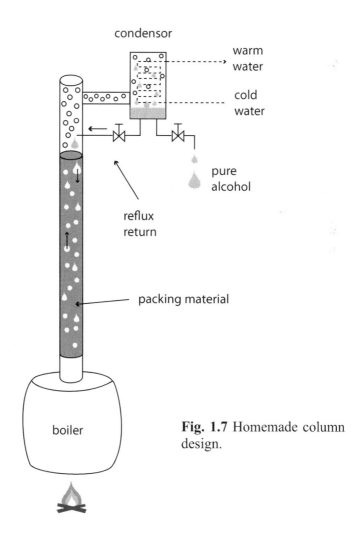

Fig. 1.7 Homemade column design.

liquid inside the column. It should be easy to clean and should not settle or pack the column. The materials which are often used include Raschig rings, structured sheet metal, marble balls or stainless steel pads for washing dishes.

Photo 1.3 Home made columns operate on household electrical current or they can be heated with propane.

We are not going into details about building columns as our book is about making alcohol beverages. Plans for making reflux fractionating columns can be found all over the internet. The links are listed at the end of the book. If a person lives in a country where distilling alcoholic spirits is permitted, he will find enough information in our book to produce his own distilled vodkas or liqueurs. To conform to American law, those who live in the USA should produce alcohol beverages using alcohol that was legally purchased in a store.

Photo 1.4 Modern distillation column for home use. This digitally controlled distillation column is capable of producing 1 liter per hour of superb quality 95% pure alcohol. *Made by VSOP www.vsop.com.pl*

Alcohol Properties

The process of making flavored vodkas, infusions and liqueurs relies on mixing alcohol of varying strengths with fruits, herbs and juices. It is advisable to get familiar with properties of alcohol in order to choose the proper strength for a particular application. You can make some infusions and weak liqueurs using 40% vodka, but your choices will be severely restricted as most extracts and infusions that will become vodkas or liqueurs can only be made with stronger alcohols.

Drinking quality alcohol is produced from foods that contain sugar. Fruits, grains, rice, corn, and potatoes all contain sugar which is converted into alcohol by the natural process called fermentation, the same method which has been used for thousands of years to produce wine. Originally, fermentation relied on yeasts that are naturally present in fruit; now we add commercially produced yeast which makes the process more dependable and easier to control. Industrial production is based on grains or potatoes and those raw materials contain sugar rich starches. Through the process known as "mashing" starch is converted to sugar and then fermentation breaks the sugar into alcohol and carbon dioxide. This fermented must is submitted to the distillation process and 96% (192 proof) alcohol is obtained. It is then diluted with water to 95% strength and distributed for general use.

The fermentation equation for breaking sugar:

$C_6H_{12}O_6$ (glucose and fructose, 100 g) $\rightarrow$ $2C_2H_5OH$ (ethyl alcohol, 51 g) $+$ $2C_2O_2$ (carbon dioxide, 49 g)

One may say the more sugar the fruit contains, the more alcohol will be obtained. How about fermenting pure table sugar, isn't it loaded with alcohol? Well those statements hold true, however, there are some limitations to making alcohol from heavy sugar syrup. As the yeasts produce more and more alcohol, a point is reached *when the alcohol will start killing them.* That may happen at around 14-18% alcohol, depending on the resistance of the yeast strain. They will die even if there is still unfermented sugar remaining in the must. *This sugar will be wasted.* This is the reason why we cannot produce stronger wines stronger than 16-18%, unless we add pure alcohol to them. As the majority of fruits contain between 7-12% sugar, yeast should be able to convert this sugar into alcohol. However, we often add more sugar on purpose into a wine must. The yeast will die before all the sugar can be converted into alcohol. They will sink to the bottom becoming a sediment.

From now on we will define the strength of alcohol in percent by volume (%ABV) and not in proofs as the latter method is practiced mainly in the USA. To convert percent into proof multiply by 2, for example: 40% alcohol (45%) = 40 x 2 = 80-proof. Pure drinking quality alcohol contains 95% alcohol which is equivalent to 190 proof.

Pure Alcohol

Ethanol (pure alcohol) is a hydrophilic organic solvent, i.e. it mixes readily with water and various water solutions like sugar syrup, but it will not mix directly with sugar. This statement applies to 95% pure drinking quality alcohol. The maximum strength of alcohol that can be produced by the *distillation process* alone is 97.2% alcohol. The remaining 2.8% water cannot be separated from alcohol as it forms with alcohol as an azeotrope. *From Wikipedia*: "An azeotrope is a mixture of two or more liquids in such a ratio that its composition cannot be changed by simple distillation. This occurs because when an azeotrope is boiled, the resulting vapor has the same ratio of constituents as the original mixture.

This water can be further removed by adding chemicals, something which must not be performed by a hobbyist as a dangerous and unsafe type of alcohol may be obtained. Such 99.5% (199 proof) alcohols are added to gasoline mixtures to remove water and to increase the octane number of the fuel. The strength of alcohol influences its other characteristics such as the amount of water, boiling temperature (78.3-100° C) and specific gravity (0.794-1.0). Alcohol is an extremely volatile liquid that burns with a light bluish flame.

Many traditional recipes call for fruit, 95% alcohol, sugar and water. Sugar and water are mixed first to create syrup and only then this syrup will combine with alcohol. However, there are different strengths of alcohol. For example if we add 390 ml of water to 1 liter of 95% alcohol, we will obtain an alcohol solution of about 70%. There is already some water present so obviously such a weaker version of alcohol can bind some sugar. Sugar has limited solubility in pure ethanol, but the 40% vodka contains 60% water and can dissolve an appreciable amount of sugar. Hence vodka may be diluted with whatever watery beverage you desire to use, in whatever proportions. If too much sugar is added, then undissolved crystals will remain. Skilled manipulation at different temperatures of the solubility properties of 40% ethanol may result in the formation of large, nice-looking sugar crystals in the bottle.

An interesting property of alcohol is it dissolves organic oils and fats. On the other hand oils and water do not mix well. You should realize that if pure alcohol was mixed with nuts it probably dissolved some oils, yet the alcohol solution is clear. We would normally make such a solution weaker by adding some water. When water is added, the alcohol may be diluted to such a degree that it can no longer hold the oil in solution. The problem may not be immediately noticeable, but in a few days the product may become cloudy. A good example is the preparation of the French aperitif Pernod. Star anise oil is diluted in 40% alcohol (vodka), forming a clear, yellow solution. When people add water to the drink a whitish emulsion of small undissolved oil drops suddenly appear making Pernod look like yellowish milk.

USA Alcohol Restrictions

Here in the USA we have a little dilemma as far as obtaining pure alcohol is concerned. Pure, drinking quality alcohol (95%) was imported from Poland for many years. It is called "Spirytus" and it can still be obtained in some states. The same applies to American made pure alcohol (95%, 190-proof) called "Everclear®." Due to its high alcohol content, 95% Everclear® and 95% Spirytus are illegal, unavailable, or difficult to find in many areas. At present, in the United States it is illegal to sell the 190-proof variety in California, Florida, Virginia, Maryland, Washington, and West Virginia. In Canada, 95% alcohol is sold in the province of Alberta, but not in most other provinces. In British Columbia it is available for purchase with a permit for medical use, research use, or industrial use only. Some municipalities, such as Chicago, have banned sales of 95% alcohol to the general public even though the state permits it to be sold.

The reason is that some college students were getting dangerously drunk drinking plain 90-95% alcohol. Yes, one can drink pure alcohol and the experience should last a lifetime. It takes some skill to handle such liquor and usually newcomers are introduced to the skill by older friends. Unfortunately, some students were showing off their drinking prowess and did not realize the potency of pure alcohol. Many ended up in hospitals and that led to the ban. This miniature prohibition should not affect our efforts of making good tinctures at home as 75% (151-proof) Everclear® made by Luxco® is available everywhere.

Diluting Alcohol

It does not matter whether water is poured into alcohol or vice versa. Alcohol is lighter than water (1 liter of alcohol weighs 790 g, 1 liter of water weighs 1000 g) but it dissolves in water easily. It is an extremely flammable liquid so exercise caution. Stay away from flames and heat sources. After the solution has been made, check the strength with an alcohol tester, if you have one.

Example A: you have 1 liter of 95% alcohol and you need 70% alcohol for infusion. How much water is needed? Locate the 70% column and the cell under says that 391 milliliters of water are needed. If you add 391 ml of water, you will obtain 1.391 liter of 70% alcohol.

Example B: you have 1 liter of 75% alcohol and you need 45% alcohol. How much water is needed? Locate the 45% column and the cell under says that 690 milliliters of water are needed. If you add 690 ml of water, you will obtain 1.690 liter of 70% alcohol. Of course if you halve the amounts, e.g. 0.5 liter 75% alcohol and 345 ml of water, you will also obtain 45% alcohol solution.

Table 1.1

To make **1 liter** of desired alcohol	Mix	
	75% Alcohol	Water
40%	533 ml	467 ml
50%	667 ml	333 ml
60%	800 ml	200 ml
70%	933 ml	67 ml

Often, the recipe will call for smaller volumes, for example 200 ml, 300 ml or 450 ml. The data can be easily calculated from the above table but we make it even simpler by creating table 1.4.

Table 1.2 The following table states how much water must be added to 1 liter of 95% alcohol in order to obtain alcohol of the desired strength.

The amount of water that must be added to **1 liter of 95% alcohol** in order to obtain new strength (at 20° C, 68° F)

90%	85%	80%	75%	70%	65%	60%	55%	50%	45%	40%	35%	30%	25%	20%
63 ml	130 ml	209 ml	294 ml	391 ml	501 ml	629 ml	779 ml	957 ml	1.17 liter	1.44 liter	1.78 liter	2.23 liter	2.87 liter	3.81 liter

Table 1.3 The following table states how much water must be added to **1 liter of 75% alcohol** in order to obtain alcohol of the desired strength.

The amount of water that must be added to 1 liter of 75% alcohol in orer to obtain new strength (at 20° C, 68° F)

70%	65%	60%	55%	50%	45%	40%	35%	30%	25%	20%
70 ml	150 ml	250 ml	360 ml	520 ml	690 ml	900 ml	1.17 liter	1.53 liter	2.03 liter	2.78 liter

Table 1.4

To make **100 ml** of desired alcohol	Mix	
	75% Alcohol	Water
40%	53.3 ml	46.7 ml
50%	66.7 ml	33.3 ml
60%	80 ml	20 ml
70%	93.3 ml	6.7 ml

Let's assume you need 300 ml of 50% alcohol. Well, take the volume that is needed for 100 ml and multiply by a 3. In this case we need 3 x 66.7 ml of 75% alcohol and 3 x 33.3 ml of water.

200.1 + 99.9 = 300 ml of 50% alcohol.

We can calculate any amount by multiplying the 100 ml of desired alcohol by a corresponding factor. For example we need 750 ml of 60% alcohol. Our factor is 7.5 as 7.5 x 100 ml comes to 750 ml.

7.5 x 80 + 7.5 x 20 = 600 + 150 = 750 ml of 60% alcohol.

The Magic Equation

Often an old recipe calls for 95% alcohol, but we only have 75% alcohol or 40% vodka. We know that we would need more of a weaker alcohol, but by how much? The magic equation comes to the rescue:

C1 x V1 = C2 x V2
C1 – the strength of the alcohol that we should have
V1 – the volume of the alcohol that we should have
C2 – the strength of the alcohol that we will use instead
V2 – the volume of the alcohol that we will use instead

Example A: the recipe calls for 1 liter of 95% alcohol, but we have only 75% alcohol at hand. How much 75% alcohol do we need?

C1 = 95, V1 = 1 liter, C2 = 75, V2 = ?
C1 x V1 = C2 x V2
V2 = C1 x V1/C2
V2 = 95 x 1 /75
V2 = 95 x 0.013
V2 = 1.26 liter

To replace 1 liter of 95% alcohol we have to use 1.26 liters of 75% alcohol.

We need more 75% alcohol because water was added to 95% alcohol to bring it down to make the 75% version. And how much water? All we have to do is to subtract the volume of 95% alcohol from the volume of 75% alcohol, in this case: 1.26 – 1.00 = 0.26 l = 260 ml.

Table 1.2 asks for 294 ml which is 26 ml more than our calculation, but our result is sufficient for home production. Keep in mind that the alcohol tables are very accurate and they include corrections for alcohol contraction and temperature.

It does not matter whether we use liters, milliliters, 95% or 0.95 as long as we use the same criteria for both sides of the equation. This is a very simple equation to solve that most people should be familiar with.

Example B: the recipe calls for 500 ml of 40% alcohol (vodka strength), but we have only 75% alcohol. How much 75% alcohol do we need?

$C_1 = 75, V_1 = ?, C_2 = 40, V_2 = 500$ ml
$C_1 \times V_1 = C_2 \times V_2$
$V_1 = C_2 \times V_2/C_1$
$V_1 = 0.40 \times 500/0.75$
$V_1 = 200/0.75$
$V_1 = 266$ ml

We can replace 500 ml of 40% alcohol with 266 ml of 75% alcohol.

This is a wonderful equation that allows us to switch over between different alcohol strengths.

Example C: You have 1 liter of 75% alcohol and you need 60% alcohol for a fruit infusion. You know that if you start adding water to 75% alcohol you will reach a point when 60% alcohol will be obtained. That could be done by using an alcohol tester. However, it would be nice to know beforehand how much water is needed. Let's start with the equation:

$C_1 = 0.75, V_1 = 1$ liter, $C_2 = 0.60, V_2 = ?$
$C_1 \times V_1 = C_2 \times V_2$
$V_2 = C_1 \times V_1/C_2$
$V_2 = 0.75 \times 1/0.60$
$V_2 = 0.75/0.60$
$V_2 = 1.25$ liter

The answer says that you can replace 1 liter of 75% alcohol with 1.25 liter of 60% alcohol. However, you want to know how much water should be added to 75% alcohol.

The amount of alcohol *has not changed.* You have 1000 ml (1 liter) of 75% alcohol which is a mixture of pure alcohol with water. This means that you have 75% of pure alcohol and 25% of water:

0.75 x 1000 = 750 ml
This is the amount of pure alcohol.
0.25 x 1000 = 250 ml
This is the amount of water.

If you add water to this solution, the volume of the solution will increase, but *the volume of alcohol remains the same,* as alcohol did not go anywhere. *The difference is the extra amount of added water.*

Because the equation says that you need 1.25 liter of 60% alcohol and the original amount of 75% alcohol was 1 liter, the difference is the added water: 1.25 – 1.00 = 0.25 liter (250 ml). The conclusion is that if you add 250 ml of water to 1 liter 75% alcohol you will obtain 1.25 liter of 60% alcohol. If you look at Table 1.3 you will see that it agrees with the data.

Let's modify the equation so we can calculate water directly from the equation:

Let x = amount of water to be added, and let's calculate the amount of alcohol in the mixture before and after the water is added. Since you are only adding water, *the amount of alcohol before equals the amount of alcohol after,* and this is basis for the equation.

Amount of alcohol before = 0.75 x 1 liter
Adding x liters of water (no alcohol)
Amount of alcohol after = 0.60 x (1 liter + x)

Equation:

C1 x V1 = C2 x (C1 + x)
C1 x V1/C2 = C1 + x
C1 x V1/C2 – C1 = x
0.75 x 1/0.60 – 1 = x
0.75/0.60 – 1 = x
1.25 – 1 = 0.25
X = 0.25 liter (250 ml) of water.

Check:

Beginning alcohol = 0.75 (1 liter) = 0.75 liter
After water added, alcohol = 0.60 (1 + 0.25) = 0.60 x 1.25 = 0.75 liter

The amount of alcohol before equals the amount of alcohol after. What has changed is the amount of water.

Alcohol Volume Contraction

Mixing water with alcohol creates a phenomenon known as volume contraction. Water molecules force their way through alcohol particles and this amount of friction generates heat and a corresponding 9-12° C increase in temperature. This also results in about a 3-5% reduction in volume. Because of this volume contraction, diluting alcohol with water does not follow linear proportions. This means that adding 1000 ml of water to 1000 ml 95% alcohol will not result in a 2000 ml solution. What we get is 1,928 ml of 45% alcohol as 72 ml has disappeared because of volume contraction. It sounds illogical but it is true and can be verified with any measuring cylinder. This "loss" is compensated by adding 72 ml water. To make matters worse alcohol is very sensitive to temperature changes and bottling alcohol at different temperatures produces different volumes which may result in a financial gain or loss for the manufacturer. Because of that the industry uses alcohol tables that provide readings of volumes of different strength alcohols at different temperatures.

Make note that when you mix alcohol with water you have to deal with alcohol contraction which was explained earlier. That is why your results may slightly differ from the data in alcohol tables. Alcohol contraction is of utmost importance for commercial producers who make thousands of liters of alcohol every hour. For a hobbyist the results obtained by using the equation are fine.

Pure alcohol is made from:

- Grains - barley, corn.
- Sugar beets.
- Potatoes.

It is usually made in 95% or extremely pure 96.5% grade. The latter is used for making superior quality vodkas like Polish Wyborowa.

Although distilling alcohol is illegal at home, there are many operators who make it either for their own use or for selling for profit. They usually choose sugar as the raw material for the following reasons:

- It is relatively inexpensive.
- Mixes readily with water.
- Produces plenty of alcohol.
- Using proper yeasts sugar ferments within 3 days.
- It does not require special containers.
- Does not produce heavy odors.

We are not going to go into the distillation process or into building distilling columns at home for two reasons:

- It is illegal to distill alcoholic spirits at home.
- It requires expensive equipment and a lot of outside space.

Understanding the behavior and properties of alcohol is crucial for making good spirits. Think of alcohol as a versatile tool that you use for making drinks. By intelligent manipulation of the properties of alcohol, you will create top quality drinks and you will be able to control their strengths. As the chapters unfold the reader will see how to choose different alcohols for different applications.

Chapter 2

Materials, Ingredients
and Equipment

Fruit

Fully ripened fresh fruit contains the most sugar, juice and the strongest aroma. Any damaged, partly fermented or suspicious fruit must be discarded as it will adversely affect the quality of the product.

Frozen fruit is fine as freezing preserves the original quality of the fruit, and, the expanding ice crystals damage the fruit's cell structure which contributes to a strong juice extract later in the maceration process.

Wild fruit is also fine. It may produce less juice than a garden variety, but it exhibits a stronger flavor and color, and also contains more aromatic substances. This can be attributed to the fact that wild growing fruit is generally smaller, and contains proportionally more skin relative to its flesh. The substances which are responsible for the color, flavor and aroma of the fruit are mainly located in the skin. Green unripe walnuts make one of the most popular Polish infusions (Orzechowka - nut cordial).

Dry fruit such as prunes, raisins or figs contain little moisture but retain almost all of the original flavor and aroma compounds. Dry plums will produce clearer infusions than fresh ones. *Avoid prunes which carry a smoky flavor.* Dry citrus skins deliver a wonderful aroma and produce clear vodkas.

All fruits are suitable for making infusions:

Fruits with pits – plums, sour cherries, cherries, peaches, apricots. Pits are discarded as they may contain traces of cyanide which exhibits an intense odor of bitter almonds. However, if the dosage is properly administered, this aroma contributes positively to the overall flavor of the drink. The accepted practice is to retain about 20-25% of pits in relation to the weight of the fruit base. For example pitted tart (sour) cherries make great infusions, but if 20% of pits are added to the must, the infusion becomes simply superb, displaying a delicate touch of an almond aroma.

Fruits with seeds – apples, oranges, pears, quinces, wild rose, dogwood, and hawthorn. Most seeds should be removed as they generally impart a bitter taste. Seeds from apples, oranges or pears contain pectin which develops cloudiness in the juice.

Berries – blackberries, black and red currants, raspberries, strawberries, rowan, gooseberries, elderberries. Berries make great alcoholic beverages.

Fruits contain plenty of water, 82-88%, the rest are sugars (5-10%), ash (0.3-0.7%), pectin (0.2-1%) acids (0.2-3%) and cellulose (0.3-5%). Fruit that grows in warmer climates is generally sweeter, for example Polish plums may contain 10% sugar, but the same variety grown in Bulgaria contains 15-20% sugar. Oranges that are grown in Europe, Florida or California will also exhibit some differences.

Fruit Name	% Water	% Sugar
Apple	85.56	10.39
Apricot	86.35	9.24
Banana	74.91	12.23
Black berries	88.15	4.88
Black currants	81.96	7.00
Blue berries	84.21	9.96
Cherries	91.41	7.69
Cranberries	87.13	4.04
Grapes	81.30	16.25
Grapefruit	90.48	7.31
Lemon	88.98	2.50
Mandarin	85.17	10.58
Orange	86.75	9.35
Papaya	88.06	7.82
Passion fruit	72.93	11.20
Peach	88.87	8.39
Pear	83.71	9.80
Pineapple	86.00	9.85
Plums	87.23	9.92
Prunes (dry plums)	30.92	38.13
Raisins, seedless	15.43	59.19
Raspberries	85.75	4.42
Sour cherries	86.13	8.49
Strawberries	90.95	4.89
Above data from the US National Nutrient Database		

Fruit Preparation

- Fruit must be washed. Soft, delicate fruits such as raspberries are generally not washed as they will lose too much juice. They may be showered cautiously taking care not to agitate the skin.

- Fruit is broken, smashed into smaller parts which breaks cell and skin structure, facilitating juice extraction. However, fruit should not be pulverized in a food processor as this will produce a cloudier juice.

Depending on the ease of obtaining juice, the fruit can be classified into two groups:

1. Apples, grapes, strawberries, sour cherries – fruits that either contain little pectin, or have pectin that does not readily dissolve in water. Those fruits leave a lot of pulp and release a relatively clear juice.

2. Apricots, black currants, raspberries, plums, peaches, citrus and other tropical fruit – these fruits contain a harder skin and pectin that does not dissolve easily in water.

The fruit from the second group is usually prepared for juicing by:

A. Breaking it into smaller particles and resting them for 4-12 hours. This starts pectin reactions which soften the skin and helps to recover more juice.

B. Commercial producers add specially prepared enzymes which help extract more juice.

Commercial presses are very efficient and will deliver from 60 – 80% juice in relation to the weight of material.

Alcohol Fruit Juice

If freshly obtained juice will be stored, it is mixed with alcohol to obtain a 16-20% alcoholic solution. This amount of alcohol will preserve the juice by preventing natural yeasts from starting fermentation. Such alcohol preserved juice is known in Poland as *fruit mors*. Commercial producers mix those alcohol preserved juices with essential oils, alcohol, syrups, infusions and other ingredients when they compose a new drink.

The amount of particular alcohol that is needed to produce alcohol juice at a certain strength can be easily calculated using the following equation:

$$X = A \times s/(S-s)$$

X – the needed amount of alcohol that would be added to juice.

A – the amount of juice that would be mixed with alcohol.

S – the strength of alcohol that would be added to juice.

s- the strength of alcohol juice that would be obtained.

Example: we have 75% alcohol and we want to produce 1 liter of alcohol juice at 19%.

Solution: 1 x 19/(75-19) = 19/56 = 0.339 1 = 340 ml

If we mix 340 ml of 75% alcohol with 1 l juice we will obtain alcohol juice at 19% alcohol strength.

Using 95% Alcohol			Using 75% Alcohol		
Alcohol	Fruit juice	Alcohol juice strength	Alcohol	Fruit juice	Alcohol juice strength
250 ml	1000 ml	19%	340 ml	1000 ml	19%
200 ml	1000 ml	16%	270 ml	1000 ml	16%

Alcohol juice is usually made by mixing 0.25 liter 95% alcohol with 1 liter of juice in a 1:4 ratio. As in most places in the USA the strongest obtainable alcohol is 75%, the proportion becomes: *1 liter of juice to 340 ml 75° alcohol.* In both cases the resulting drinks contain about 19% of alcohol. Alcohol juice is often made from the leftover liquid after the second infusion. Such preserved fresh juice is stored for up to 12 months for later use as a component of flavored spirits. Naturally, it is delicious to drink at any time.

Freshly produced alcohol juice should not be used for 14-30 days. Alcohol tends to extract microscopic particles such as pectin, tannin, proteins, etc. Those particles need some time to sink to the bottom and produce a clear juice. This is the same process as clarifying wine. After that period the clear juice is siphoned and the sediment discarded. Even after all those procedures certain juices like plum or lemon may still remain cloudy.

Infusions

Although infusions hold their own right as a type of alcoholic spirits, they may also be considered a material that can be blended with alcohol for making flavored vodkas. They may be the main ingredient or the supplementary one. Infusions are wonderful materials, however, their production requires so much time and space that commercial producers tend to stay away from them. The industry prefers to use alcohol juices. Infusions, however, are clearer and more flavorsome than alcohol juices and a hobbyist can use them for making a variety of sophisticated blends.

Fruits such as blackthorn, rowan, bird cherry, and hawthorn contain a large pit but little flesh. Obtaining juice from such fruits by pressing is difficult and infusion produces the best results.

Essential Oils

Natural essential oils can be added as a primary or supplemental flavor. They have a very strong taste and flavor and are usually added at 1-2 ml (0.01-0.02%) per 10 liter of product. For example, 1 ml of orange oil is enough to make 10 liters of orange flavored vodka. Sometimes we may use oil to enhance the flavor of the infusion and only 0.1 ml is needed for 10 liters of liquid. If only one liter of infusion is made, this number becomes 10 times smaller. Wonderful orange vodkas can be made by combining orange skin infusion with orange essential oil.

Most essential oils come in a 10-30 ml bottle with a dropper, but administering such small amounts of oil is still difficult. An easy solution is to mix oil with 10 times more alcohol. For example 1 ml of oil is measured with a pipette and placed in a measuring cylinder. Next 9 ml of pure alcohol is added creating 10 ml of oil in the alcohol solution. Now, if we need to add 0.1 ml of oil into our 1 liter vodka, the task is much easier as we need to administer 1 ml of the solution.

An even easier solution can be made by mixing 1 ml of oil with 99 ml of 95% alcohol. What we get is a 100 ml solution with 1 ml of oil inside. To administer 0.1 ml of oil, we need to remove 10 ml of the solution and that becomes quite easy.

Finding essential oil that is suitable for making beverages can be confusing. After doing much research we have finally discovered Mountain Rose Herbs www.mountainroseherbs.com. This company offers not only great essential oils but an impressive collection of herbs as well.

Photo 2.1 An essential oil and eye dropper with its bottle.

There are hundreds of essential oils which are used in therapeutic aromatherapy applications and many of them are suitable for making alcoholic spirits. Keep in mind that stronger alcohol yields better oil dissolution. Oils will dissolve well in 96% alcohol, but in alcohols weaker than 55% dissolution becomes negligible. During the composition of a new alcoholic spirit the essential oils must be added to alcohol first, dissolved and only then juices, syrup and water may be introduced. Essential oils should be kept in dark bottles in cool areas and used within 6 months. They lose their quality when exposed to light, air and warm temperatures.

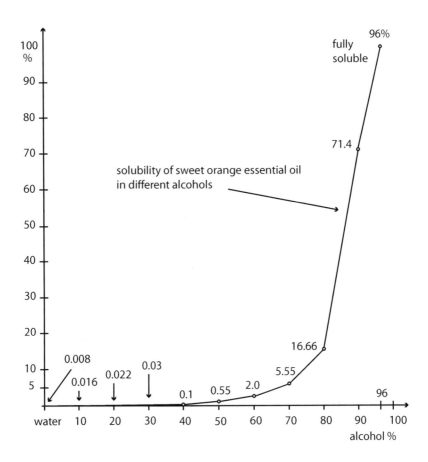

Fig. 2.1 Solubility of sweet orange essential oil in different alcohols.

It can be seen in the graph that the ability of oil to dissolve in alcohol decreases drastically when the strength of alcohol drops below 80%.

Photo 2.2 About 3 ml of orange oil in different alcohols (from left to right: 40%, 75%, 95%).

If you decide to experiment with essential oils follow these steps:

- Don't add essential oil directly into drinks.
- Add a drop of oil to the strongest alcohol you are going to use.
- Mix well together.
- Pour the oil/alcohol solution into the spirit you are making and stir well. The solution should remain clear.

Adding 1 ml of good quality essential oil directly to 40% alcohol (vodka) does not create any cloudiness. Cloudiness starts to appear at about 2 ml/l. Applying more than 2 ml/l will make the drink taste unpleasant and cloudy. Stir the solution by shaking the bottle vigorously.

Water

Good quality tap water is fine. There are hard waters that contain large amounts of calcium (Ca) or magnesium (Mg) and those should be avoided, especially when used for cooling distillate, as calcium would accumulate on pipes in the form of stone. Secondly, they may add a degree of cloudiness to the finished product which is noticeable only after a few days or even weeks. A common soap does not want to foam well in hard water and that is quite a reliable test. If in doubt, use inexpensive distilled water which does not contain any minerals that could affect the flavor of the product. Water is usually treated with chlorine and sometimes the smell of chlorine may be noticeable. Boiling such water will eliminate this odor.

Sugar

Refined white sugar, whether cane or from sugar beets is fine. Adding brown sugar to light colored beverages should be avoided as it may darken your product. Sugar is diluted in water first and only then added to the fruit mixture. *Pure alcohol does not mix with sugar, but will mix with sugar syrup.* Sugar (sucrose) molecules are polar; they have a positive and a negative end. Water molecules have the same property. For this reason, the positive end of a sugar molecule will be attracted to the negative end of a water molecule and dissolve. Alcohols are non-polar and are *equally* charged on all sides. The charged ends of the sucrose have nothing to be attracted to except other sugar molecules, therefore they will not dissolve in pure alcohol.

There is a limit to the maximum amount of sugar that can dissolve in a given volume of water and this is known as a saturated solution. Adding more sugar will result in sinking it to the bottom and will create an unappetizing drink. This is dependent on the volume and temperature of water. Browne in his "Handbook of Sugar Analysis" states that, at 20° C (68° F), 204 grams of sugar is soluble in 100 ml of water. Thus, at 68° F room temperature about 2 grams of sucrose is soluble in 1 ml of water. At 100° C 487 grams of sucrose is soluble in 100 ml of water.

Solubility of Sucrose in Water at Different Temperatures		
Degrees °C	Degrees °F	Grams of sucrose dissolved by 100 g (100 ml) of water
0 (freezing point)	32	179.2
10	50	190.5
20	68	203.9
30	86	219.5
40	104	238.1
50	122	260.4
60	140	287.3
70	158	320.5
80	176	362.1
90	194	415.7
100 (boiling point)	212	487.2

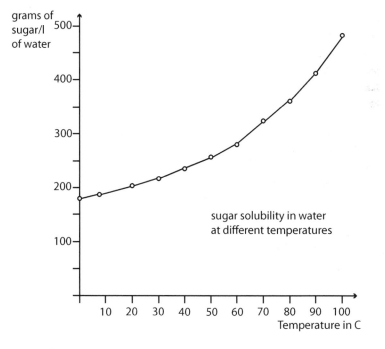

Fig 2.2 Solubility of sugar in water.

Sugar Syrup

As mentioned above, pure alcohol will not mix with sugar but will mix with sugar syrup. You can dilute 2 kg of sugar in 1 kg of (1 liter) water at room temperature. You can dilute even more sugar in warm water but there is a danger of sugar coming out of the solution when the solution cools down. To prevent this, add a small amount of citric acid (0.08%) or a few drops of lemon juice and boil the syrup for 10-15 minutes. Remove any foam that forms on top. The syrup is stabilized now and sugar will not come out of the solution.

Different sugar syrups can be produced but the following combination saves a lot of time and calculations. Commercial producers like to use 73% sugar syrup (1 kg sugar and 400 ml water) for two reasons:

- Such heavy syrup can be stored for a number of weeks without the risk of developing mold.

- One milliliter of 73% sugar syrup weighs 1 gram. Such syrup is of immense help for making sweet vodkas and liqueurs. Let's say that the recipe asks for 400 g of sugar per 1 liter of liqueur. All we have to do is to pour 400 milliliters of syrup and the required amount of sugar has been added. There is no need to use a scale, no need to mix, it is clear and ready.

Procedure:

Add sugar slowly to 80° C, 176° F water and mix thoroughly. At 20° C (68° F) sugar becomes saturated at 892 g/1000 ml of water so adding 1000 g/400 ml of water will cross the limit and sugar will come out of the solution when it cools down. To prevent this around 0.08% (0.8 g per 1 kg of sugar) of citric acid is added and the syrup is boiled for 15 minutes. When sugar is completely dissolved in water and the syrup is clear, remove from heat. Cooking syrup too long will result in a yellowish color. After cooling *the sugar will not come out of the solution*. If you like to be exact, you may check your syrup; you know that you have mixed 1 kg of sugar with 420 ml of water (extra 20 ml covers boiling loss) but your measuring cylinder says that you have only 975 ml of syrup. Well, you have lost more water during boiling than anticipated so add 25 ml more to make it 1 liter.

Syrup	Amount of water added to 1 kg of sugar in ml	Amount of syrup in ml	Amount of sugar in 1 liter of syrup in g	Specific gravity at 15° C
73%	400*	1000	1000	1.370
60%	670*	1250	780	1.290

* You may add an extra 20-50 ml of water to compensate for the boiling loss. 73% sugar syrup is often called normal sugar syrup.

Many infusion recipes call for mixing equal amounts of sugar with water, i.e. ½ liter of water with ½ kg of sugar. Syrup with such a low sugar concentration must be used within days, otherwise mold will grow and the solution will spoil. Obviously, such an arrangement cannot be accepted by commercial producers who like to keep a large amount of sugar syrup at hand.

If you plan to make sweet vodkas and liqueurs often, preparing syrup in advance is the way to go. Imagine making 1 liter of liqueur nine times in one month. The recipe will call for let's say 450 g of sugar. This means you will have to measure water and sugar, boil the syrup, cool it and wash the dishes nine times. This amounts to many hours of work. It is much easier to get one big pot, pour 1.6 liters of water, add 4 kg of sugar, 3 grams of citric acid and boil it for 15 minutes. There is enough syrup for 9 liters of liqueur; it is ready to be used at a moment's notice and it blends with juice or vodka instantly. And you wash the dishes only once.

There are recipes such as Amaretto and Kahlua that ask for brown sugar. Brown sugar has a nicer flavor, but often is not as refined as the white one. This is why all surface foam should be scooped up when heating sugar syrup. In addition its brown color eliminates its use in clear spirits. It can be used for making dark drinks like chocolate or coffee liqueurs. Brown 73% sugar syrup: 300 g brown sugar, 700 g white sugar, 420 ml water, 0.8 g citric acid. The procedure for making 73% brown sugar syrup follows the steps which were outlined for making white syrup.

Photo 2.3 Impurities accumulate as foam on the surface.

Photo 2.4 Surface foam.

Photo 2.5 White sugar syrup left, brown sugar syrup right.

Photo 2.6 Ready to use 73% sugar syrup.

Vanilla Sugar

Vanilla sugar (German: Vanill-ezucker, Polish: Cukier wanilio-wy, Swedish: "Vaniljsocker") is a commonly used ingredient of German, Polish, Swedish, Finn-ish, Danish, Austrian, Norwe-gian, Czech, Slovak, Slovenian, Croatian and other European desserts.

Vanilla sugar is made of sugar, with vanilla beans or mixed with vanilla extract. It can be costly and difficult to obtain outside Europe but can be simply made at home. Vanilla sugar is easy to make, cheap and versatile. There are many uses for vanilla sugar. Essentially, it can be used in place of regular sugar for making hot

Photo 2.7 Homemade vanilla sugar.

drinks and desserts. Vanilla sugar can be added to any recipe that calls for sugar and vanilla. For example Porter Vodka is made with vanilla, sugar or honey. Egg crème is made with vanilla and plenty of sugar. Vanilla sugar fits perfectly into this recipe.

How to Make Vanilla Sugar

Vanilla sugar is very easy to make and requires nothing more than a jar, some fine sugar and vanilla pods. Vanilla sugar can be prepared at home by combining approximately 2 cups of white sugar (400 g) with the scraped seeds of one vanilla bean or one vanilla pod (3 g). Put a vanilla pod into a jar. Split vanilla pods and cut them into 2 to 3 sections. Place in a jar, fill to the top with sugar and shake well. Keep in a cool, dark and dry place, ensuring the lid is airtight. For the best flavor leave it a week before first using. As you use the sugar, replace it with more and shake before putting away. The sugar will keep indefinitely and the pods will need to be replaced annually. Once you use it you might wonder how you ever managed without it.

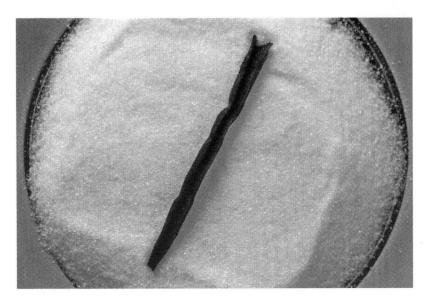

Photo 2.8 Split vanilla stick and sugar.

Caramel

Caramel is the main colorant used in production of alcoholic spirits. The range of colors it produces varies from light yellow, yellow, light brown, brown and dark brown. It is obtained by burning *white* sugar which starts to melt at 160° C (320° F). Quality caramel is made at 180-195° C (356 - 383° F). Burning it at lower temperatures produces caramel with a weak color, going over 200° C (393° F) may burn it so much that little charcoal pieces may come out of the solution, which will be noticeable in a clear spirit.

Procedure:

Keep hot water ready on a stove.

1. Heat a pan over small heat for a few minutes and then scatter ½ cup of sugar (3.8 oz, 102 g) on the bottom. Spread it equally.

2. Heat the sugar until it starts turning brown, keep on stirring using a wooden spoon. Continue melting the sugar, stirring often until it liquefies and acquires a deep golden color.

If you see the smoke or smell burnt sugar lift the pan and lower the heat. Remove from heat and let cool to about 60° C (140° F).

3. Start adding hot water slowly, continuously stirring the mixture with a wooden spoon. Place the pan back on the burner and simmer until caramel syrup is obtained. If you add 100 ml water to 100 g of caramelized sugar you will obtain syrup, but it will harden when it cools down. If you want liquid caramel syrup, you will have to add more water.

Photo 2.9 Melting sugar.

Photo 2.10 Melting sugar.

Photo 2.11 Melting sugar.

Photo 2.12 Melting sugar.

Photo 2.13 Rock caramel, caramel candy.

Photo 2.14 Different caramel solutions. Left - 0.5% caramel, light yellow color, middle - 1.0%, yellow color, right - 2%, light brown color.

Caramel is the universal colorant for alcoholic drinks. It is quite powerful, you need just a little of caramel syrup or hard caramel to color the drink. Syrup will dissolve faster, but caramel rock will dissolve as well, after all it is just sugar.

Notes:

- If sugar crystals form during the final heating discard them.

- The darker the color, the more bitter your coloring will be.

- Do not use non-stick or lined copper saucepans.

Photo 2.15 Dissolving rock caramel in water.

- Use caution as hot burnt sugar can boil violently when water is added. Take the pot off the heat, let it cool and don't stand over it while adding water. Don't get hot caramel on your skin or finger; it is a sticky substance and hard to remove.

Colorants

- Caramel delivers strong yellow-light brown color. This is the most universally applied colorant.

- Saffron makes rice yellow. It delivers strong yellow color to lemon vodka or to herb infusions.

- Bilberries (European Blueberries) – deliver deep red or burgundy color.

There is confusion between European (*Vaccinium myrtillus*) bilberry and American (*Vaccinium cyanococcus*) blueberries. They look identical and are used for the same purposes. From Wikipedia: Since most people in the world refer to "blueberries", no matter if they mean the European blueberry *Vaccinium myrtillus* or the American blueberries, there is a lot of confusion about the two nearly identical fruit worldwide. One can distinguish bilberries or European blueberries from their American counterpart by the following differences: bilberries have *dark blue, strongly fragrant flesh*, while American blueberries have *white or translucent, mildly fragrant flesh*; the bilberries grow as single fruit on low bushes, usually wild in woods of the Northern Hemisphere, but American blueberries grow in a large bush with several fruit at once; bilberries are generally wild plants while American blueberries can be cultivated. Bilberry fruit *will stain hands, teeth and tongue deep blue or purple* while eating; it was used as a dye for food and clothes. American blueberries of section *Cyanococcus* have white flesh, thus are less staining.

Honey

Honey is a sweetener that contributes nicely to the taste and aroma. On the negative side, its price recently is so expensive that the choice between sugar and honey will largely depend on how deep your pockets are. Honey's color and flavor depends on the flower from which it originated. Similar to sugar, it also will darken if heated in a frying pan. The color can vary from light yellow to dark brown, and it will obviously influence the final color of the product. In many cases, honey is boiled first in order to remove the foam. This foam contains many small impurities, minuscule parts of bees included, which should be scooped up. There is no need to boil honey if it looks clear. Honey is often fermented to produce honey wine (mead), but that is an entirely new subject. Due to its superior flavor, it is added to high quality infusions and liqueurs.

Citric Acid

Citric acid is a natural preservative which is also used to add an acidic, or sour taste to foods and soft drinks. It is widely available in the form of white miniature crystals. Originally produced from lemon juice, it is now produced by fermenting sugars. You can substitute *0.8 g citric acid with ½ teaspoon of fresh lemon juice*. Citric acid is used widely in general cooking, wine making and is always added to honey wine, otherwise the honey will taste somewhat bland.

10 g of citric acid is diluted in 50 ml of water and poured into a measuring cylinder. Then 40% alcohol is added to the 100 ml mark and a 10% citric acid solution is obtained. One gram of citric acid corresponds to 10 ml of the solution. The solution can be measured with a cylinder or withdrawn with a syringe.

Aromatic Extracts and Infusions

Aromatic spices such as vanilla, cinnamon, nutmeg or orange and lemon skins are commonly added to many infusions and liqueurs. It makes our work much easier if strong extracts/infusions are made from those materials for future use.

Ingredient	Amount in grams	Alcohol		Macerating Time
		Strength	Amount	
Vanilla	10	50%	90 ml	3 weeks
Cinnamon	10	50%	90 ml	3 weeks
Cloves	10	50%	90 ml	3 weeks
Nutmeg	10	50%	90 ml	3 weeks
Star Anise	10	50%	90 ml	3 weeks
Almonds**	10	75%	20 ml	3 weeks
Lemon Skins*	10	75%	50 ml	3-4 days
Orange Skins*	10	75%	50 ml	3-4 days
*Remove white pith from the skin, otherwise it will impart a bitter flavor. Cut skin into smaller pieces. **Almonds are shelled, but the skin is left on. When macerating is completed, filter infusion through coffee filter.				

Spices are mixed with alcohol in a 1:9 ratio. This makes it easy to measure later. For example take 10 g of cinnamon stick. Break the stick into 1 cm pieces, then add 90 ml of 50% alcohol. After macerating, strain the liquid and place in a measuring cylinder. Add water to 100 ml mark. Now you have 100 ml solution where each 10 ml equals to 1 g of cinnamon stick. You can easily measure and apply 1 ml (0.1 g) of solution with a common syringe. Using 1:9 ratio for citrus skins and almond infusions does not produce a desired flavor so the proportions are different.

American supermarkets carry pure vanilla extract. This makes your work easier and vanilla extract can be added after the infusion has been strained and filtered.

1 g vanilla stick = about 1 ml vanilla extract

10 ml vanilla infusion = about 5 ml vanilla extract

To simplify matters you may create an All-in-One aromatic infusion that you can apply to your recipes:

Vanilla stick, 3 (around 9 g)
Cloves, 2
Cinnamon stick, about 1 cm
75% alcohol, 100 ml

1. Place all ingredients in a jar, add alcohol and macerate for 3 weeks.

2. Strain, filter and bottle.

Photo 2.16 Filtering vanilla sticks infusion.

Citrus Skins Infusion

Citrus aroma is due to the aromatic oil that the skin contains. It takes around 10 kg of skins to produce 150 g (1.5%) of the oil. The oil is retrieved by cold pressing skins using machines that are beyond the reach of an ordinary homeowner. However, homemade extracts/infusions provide good results.

Photo 2.17 Orange skins infusion.

Procedure:

Peel off the skins and remove the white pith as it is bitter. Cut skins into 1 cm pieces and cover with 75% alcohol. Macerate for 3-4 days, then filter through a coffee filter. Although basic rules state that strong alcohols should be used with juice rich fruits, in this case we are not after the juice but after the orange and lemon aromatic oils that the skins contain. Oils dissolve readily in strong alcohol and weak alcohols will not extract them well. Maceration time is 3-4 days only as the infusion will become bitter if allowed to continue longer.

Citrus fruits don't filter well, but the skins produce a very clear and aromatic infusion. Grapefruit skin infusions carry less aroma than lemon or orange infusions.

Citrus skins infusion for making vodkas:

Citrus fruit	Amount	% alcohol	Macerating time
Fresh lemon or orange skins	100 g	75%, 500 ml	3 days
Dry lemon or orange skins	50 g	50%, 500 ml	3 days

Photo 2.18 Filtering lemon skins infusion.

Herbs and Spices

The practice of using whole spices such as cloves, vanilla sticks and chopped nutmeg is encouraged as they produce little cloudiness. The best solution is to make them into an infusion which is strained, filtered and applied as needed.

Dry herbs and spices are used for making herbal infusions. Such infusions may become a part of herbal liqueurs. There are hundreds of suitable herbs and spices; the most popular follow below:

Herbs: tea, angelica root, wormwood, marjoram, basil, thyme, bison grass, lavender, linden, and elderberry flowers, and dry rose petals.

Seeds: anise, fennel, caraway, allspice, cumin, vanilla, almonds, coffee, cacao.

Tree bark: cinnamon, oak, French oak.

There are too many herbs and spices to list them all. We list only those few that are often used and we find them quite original.

Angelica archangelica. The roots and seeds are sometimes used to flavor gin. Its presence accounts for the distinct flavor of many liqueurs, such as Chartreuse and Dom Benedictine.

Cardamom *(Elettaria cardamomum)* is the world's third most expensive spice by weight, outstripped in market value only by saffron and vanilla. Cardamom has a strong, unique flavor, with an intensely aromatic, resinous fragrance. Cardamom is used as flavorings in both food and drink, as cooking spices and as a medicine. Green cardamom is used in South Asian traditional medicine to treat infections in teeth and gums, to prevent and treat throat troubles, congestion of the lungs and pulmonary tuberculosis, inflammation of eyelids as well as digestive disorders. It is also used to break up kidney stones and gall stones, and was reportedly used as an antidote for both snake and scorpion venom. For recipes requiring whole cardamom pods, a generally accepted equivalent is 10 pods equals 1½ teaspoons of ground cardamom.

Photo 2.19 Cardamom is often added to herbal liqueurs, but be aware of its power. Run a test first.

Hyssop *(Hyssopus)* is used as an ingredient in eau de Cologne and the liqueur Chartreuse. It is also used to color the spirit Absinthe, along with Melissa and Roman wormwood. Hyssop leaves have a slightly bitter minty flavor and can be added to soups, salads, or meats.

Juniper is a bush that grows everywhere in the world, including parks and streets. Its berries are added to wild game dishes, hunter's sausage, and different beverages. Gin's flavor comes chiefly from juniper. Fresh berries are green in the spring, light blue in the summer and navy blue in November. Dry berries are very dark blue and contain about 20% sugar what makes them relatively easy to ferment.

Photo 2.20 Juniper twig and dry berries.

Lemon balm *(Melissa officinalis)*, is a perennial herb in the mint family native to southern Europe and the Mediterranean region. It grows in the southern USA as well. The leaves have a gentle lemon scent, related to mint. During summer, small white flowers full of nectar appear. These attract bees, hence the genus name Melissa (Greek for 'honey bee'). Lemon balm is often used as a flavoring in ice cream and herbal teas, both hot and iced, often in combination with other herbs such as spearmint. It is also frequently added to herb infusions.

Linden Tree Flowers

Linden trees grow in Europe and in the USA. The street that leads to the famous Branderburg Gate in Berlin is called "Unter den Linden" (under linden trees). Take a cable car to Roosevelt Island in Manhattan and you see them lining up the streets. They are tall, the flowers produce a wonderful fragrance and we have been making linden tea for millennia. So next June when you pass a linden tree pick up some flowers and treat yourself to delicious tea that tastes like honey. Because of their aroma they are often added to infusions, sometimes with rose petals.

Photo 2.21 Linden flowers.

Rowan

From Wikipedia: "The European Rowan *(Sorbus aucuparia)*, a small tree typically 4–12 m tall growing in a variety of habitats throughout northern Europe and in mountains in southern Europe and southwest Asia. Its berries are a favorite food for many birds and are a traditional wild-collected food in Britain and Scandinavia. It is one of the hardiest European trees, growing even in Arctic Norway, and has also become widely naturalized in northern North America."

The encyclopedia does not mention the fact that rowan berries make one of the finest dry vodkas possible. It had been extremely popular in Poland once (Jarzebiak) and was widely distributed. Rowan berries have a tartness and a sweetness that makes them excellent for making jellies and vodka. The best time for harvest is after the first frost when berries lose their bitter taste and become slightly sweet.

Photo 2.22 Rowan tree on Polish street.

Star anise *(Illicium verum)* is used in baking as well as in liquor production, most distinctively in the production of the liquor Galliano and Sambuca, Pastis, and many types of absinthe. It goes well with peppermint and apple.

Photo 2.23 Star anise.

Sweet flag *(Acorus calamus)*, also known as Calamus is a tall perennial wetland weed. The scented leaves and more strongly scented rhizomes have traditionally been used medicinally and to make fragrances. The dried and powdered rhizome has also been used as a substitute for ginger, cinnamon and nutmeg. In Europe *Acorus calamus* was often added to wine, and the root is also one of the possible ingredients of absinthe. *Acorus calamus* is found across Europe, Southern Russia, Northern Asia Minor, Southern Siberia, China, Indonesia, Japan, Burma, Sri Lanka, Australia, as well as Southern Canada and the Northern United States. From Wikipedia: Sweet flag has been an item of trade in many cultures for thousands of years. It is widely employed in modern herbal medicine due to its sedative, laxative, diuretic, and carminative properties. It is used in Ayurvedic medicine to counter the side effects of all hallucinogens. Sweet flag is one of the most widely and frequently used herbal medicine amongst the Chipewyan people. Both roots and leaves of *A. calamus* have shown antioxidant, antimicrobial and insecticidal properties.

Photo 2.24 Sweet flag. The inner tube tastes good and can be eaten raw.

Photo 2.25 Sweet flag field in the spring.

Vanilla

Vanilla is probably the most important spice for making sweet vodkas, liqueurs and crèmes. In many countries it is available in the form of original vanilla pods which weigh about 3-4 g each. They can be added directly to infusions or a vanilla infusion can be made from them. Then the filtered vanilla infusion is added in its liquid form to any recipe that calls for vanilla. In the USA factory made natural vanilla extracts are commonly available making home production of liqueurs much simpler.

Vanilla infusion

Vanilla sticks (3), 10 g
Alcohol 70%, 90 ml

Split vanilla sticks and cut into 1 cm pieces. Macerate for 3 weeks, filter and bottle.

The 2nd infusion method

Vanilla is an expensive spice so it makes sense to retrieve as much of it as possible. The second infusion method does just that.

Vanilla, 10 g

Alcohol 70%, 70 ml

Alcohol 50%, 50 ml

1. Split vanilla sticks and cut into 1 cm pieces. Add 70 ml 70% alcohol and macerate for 3 weeks. Filter and bottle. This is your first infusion. Save vanilla cuts:

2. Add 50 ml 50% alcohol and macerate for 3 weeks. Filter and bottle.

3. Combine both vanilla infusions.

Wormwood *(Artemisia absinthium)*, is an ingredient in the spirit absinthe, and is also used for flavoring in some other spirits and wines, including bitters and vermouth. In the Middle Ages, it was used to spice mead. In 18th century England, wormwood was sometimes used instead of hops in beer. The aperitif vermouth (derived from the German word Wermut, "wormwood") is a wine flavored with aromatic herbs, but originally with wormwood. The highly potent spirits absinthe and Malört also contain wormwood. Polish vodka Zoladkowa Gorzka is flavored with wormwood. Run a test first as wormwood is very bitter.

Food Colorings

When making fruit spirits we take advantage of the natural color that those fruits, herbs and spices produce. The best additional colorings are caramel (burnt sugar) which colors drinks from light to dark brown and saffron which produces a beautiful yellow color.

Saffron

Saffron is the world's most expensive spice. It imparts a rich golden-yellow hue to dishes (yellow rice) and textiles. Add a few threads to a glass of water and in a few seconds it will be crystal clear yellow. Saffron threads can only be picked by hand and to produce 1 lb (453 g) of dry saffron we have to harvest 50,000–75,000 flowers.

Photo 2.26 Saffron and a single clove.

FDA Approved Food Colorings

The following commercially produced food colorings are approved by the USA Food and Drug Administration: Yellow 5, Red 40, Blue 1, Red 3.

More sub-colors can be obtained by combining those above colors:

Orange (yellow + red)

Purple (red + blue)

Jungle green (green = yellow)

Teal (blue + green)

Equipment

Making alcoholic spirits at home requires basic equipment such as bottles, corks, a scale and other items which are readily available in one's kitchen. A cheese cloth is handy, a measuring cylinder and scale are definitely needed. As there is no fermentation, there is no possibility of gas pressure building up inside, so a glass jar with a twisted lid can be used. This will also prevent loss of alcohol evaporation. Keep in mind that the fruits will expand in volume, so the vessels should be filled only to about 75% capacity.

Glass Jars

Make sure that your container is tight otherwise you will lose alcohol due to evaporation. Many pretty looking containers like the ones with a locking mechanism and a rubber washer are not perfectly tight and an ordinary preserve type glass jar with a twist on lid works better. Always fill it with water, flip it over and see whether it is leaking or not. This simple test can save you a lot of aggravation later.

Photo 2.27 Glass jars.

Glass jars with fruit infusions can be kept in a sunny and warm location. Glass jars with herbal infusions should be kept in a dark and cool area.

Graduated Cup and Cylinder

A graduated cylinder is used to accurately measure the volume of a liquid. A traditional cylinder is usually narrow and tall and has a "spout" for easy pouring. A cylinder without a spout will make your table wet and messy. A small 10, 25 or 50 ml cylinder is useful when measuring essential oils which are applied in very small amounts.

Photo 2.28 1800 ml graduated measuring cup.

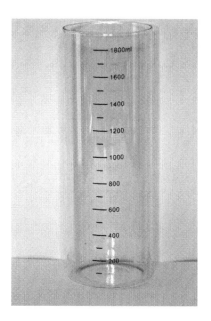
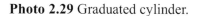

Photo 2.29 Graduated cylinder.

Photo 2.30 A small graduated 250 ml cylinder.

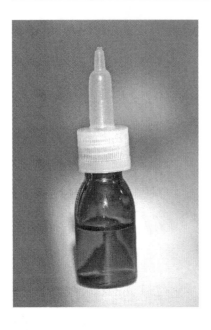

Dropper

Eye dropper with a bottle is handy when storing and applying essential oils.

Photo 2.31 Eye dropper.

Syringes

Syringes come in many sizes and allow for an accurate volume control.

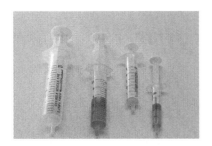

Photo 2.32 Set of syringes.

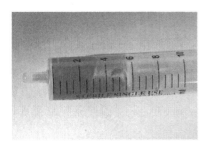

Photo 2.33 10 ml syringe is accurate to within ½ ml.

Alcohol Tester

Strong alcohol can be diluted with water to any strength by consulting alcohol tables or using basic calculations as explained in Chapter 1. However, the alcohol tester is useful for double checking calculations and is a must have tool for determining the strength of a new or unknown distillate. Alcohol volume increases with temperature. It is estimated that the volume of 1 liter of vodka increases by 1 ml with each 1° C increase in temperature. If we increase the temperature of 10 liters of vodka by 5° C its volume will increase by 50 ml, so we will have the new volume of 10,050 ml.

Alcohol testers are calibrated to give correct readings at 20° C. To compensate for alcohol volume changes with temperature a good alcohol tester has a built in thermometer with a correction factor. A reading is taken, and if the temperature is different than 20° C, the thermometer indicates how we should adjust the reading. Keep in mind that the tester is designed for solutions of alcohol and water only. It does not work when sugar, juices or infusions are added to the alcohol solution.

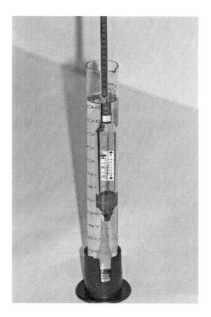

Photo 2.34 Alcohol tester in a cylinder.

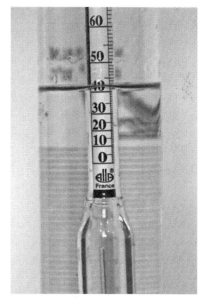

Photo 2.35 Alcohol tester – alcohol reading 42%.

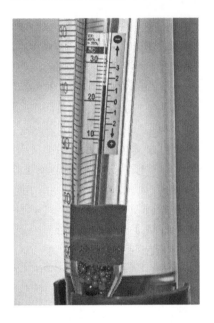

Photo 2.36 Alcohol tester – temperature reading 24° C. The correction scale indicates that the alcohol strength should be decreased by 1.5 degrees; 42 – 1.5 = 40.5. The real alcohol strength is 40.5%.

Scale

A general purpose digital scale is acceptable as long as it is accurate to within 1 gram.

When heavy sugar syrup (73%) is made about 0.7 – 0.8 g of citric acid is added to 1 kg of sugar. To measure such a small amount a highly accurate scale is needed or a solution of citric acid and water is made.

Photo 2.37 Scale.

Funnel

A few different size funnels are always handy.

Photo 2.38 Funnels.

The funnels can be lined up with a cheese cloth, medical gauze, cotton wool, coffee filter, paper towel, some even use cosmetic facial pads. Occasionally, the filtering process may proceed very slow. To prevent loss of alcohol the filter should be covered.

Photo 2.39 Filtering through a gauze in a closed jar.

Photo 2.40 Funnel covered with plate.

Sealing Bottles

The bottles which will be stored for a long time should be sealed to prevent the loss of alcohol. Bottle sealing wax comes in different colors. Place sealing wax pellets in a used metal soup can, apply heat and melt them.

Bottles With Corks. Insert cork until it is flush with the bottle. Apply some melted wax on top. Invert bottle around and dip the neck of the bottle into the melted wax. Lift up the bottle and let the wax drip down, turning the bottle around. Place the seal in cold water for 10 seconds.

Bottles with Metal Twist Caps. Apply sealing wax around the cap or dip the neck of the bottle into the melted wax. To remove the cork push your corkscrew through as though the seal wasn't even there. There is no need to scrape the wax off.

Melted candle wax is very thin, but it can be used as a last resort. Dip the neck of the bottle into melted candle wax. Remove, let cool, then dip in wax again.

Photo 2.41 Cork sealed with sealing wax.

Photo 2.42 Metal cap sealed with white candle wax.

Chapter 3

Tinctures

In chemistry, a tincture is a solution that has alcohol as the solvent. To qualify as a tincture the alcoholic extract should have an ethanol percentage of at least 40-60% (80-120 proof). In herbal medicine, alcoholic tinctures are often made with various concentrations of ethanol, 25% being the most common. The first tinctures were in reality extracts or elixirs as the first alcoholic beverages known to man were only beer and wine. The maximum alcohol content was probably around 16% since at this strength all yeasts will die and the fermentation will come to an end. Stronger spirits could only be obtained by submitting weaker spirits like wine to the distillation process, however, the process was not known yet. Herbal tinctures usually use ethanol as a solvent for people who do not consume alcohol for medical, religious or moral reasons. Non-alcoholic tinctures made with glycerin or vinegar offer an alternative, although their use is strictly limited for medicinal purposes.

The basic types of tinctures:

- Infusion
- Elixir
- Extract

Infusions are alcoholic drinks that are made by pouring alcohol over fresh or dried fruits, sometimes herbs and spices, in such a proportion that the finished product contains about 40% (80 proof) alcohol. Infusions contain all substances that fruits contain, such as vitamins, minerals, acids, sugars, pectin, aromatic oils, color agents and others. All those compounds are extracted and preserved by alcohol.

Photo 3.1 Strawberry infusion.

Some infusions include many herbs that are credited with medicinal properties and such infusions are considered to be medicinal tinctures. Alcoholic cough syrups that are sold in pharmacies are tinctures. The alcohol contained in tinctures immediately dilates the blood vessels in our body and those healing substances enter our system.

One can legally make flavored vodka or infusions at home, contrary to whiskey, rum, gin, cognac and other strong alcoholic spirits *which require distillation*. Home distillation is either prohibited in most countries (USA, Poland) or is tightly controlled (Austria).

Infusions offer many benefits because they are made with fruits, vegetables, herbs and spices. On the other hand there is no nutritional value in plain spirits like vodka, except maybe in widening the blood vessels, a fact which is generally recognized. There is no official standard for making infusions so one is not limited to the strength of alcohol or the amount of sugar it carries. They can be produced from any fruit at any desired strength. This creates unlimited possibilities for a creative person who can create drinks of many flavors and colors.

Extracts

Extract - a substance made by removing part of a raw material, often by using a solvent such as alcohol, oil or water. The majority of natural essences are obtained by extracting the essential oil from blossoms, fruit, roots, or the whole plants through pressing, absorption, maceration and distillation.

Hot water extract is the outcome of steeping dried herbs, flowers or berries in water. Water is typically boiled and then poured over the herb, which is then allowed to steep in the liquid for a period of time. The liquid may then be strained or the herbs otherwise removed from the solution. Steeping performed for no more than 15 to 30 minutes, or until the mixture cools, will create a beverage with optimal flavor. Steeping for up to four hours, however, produces stronger medical herbal infusions. A common example of a hot water infusion is *tea*. Many fruits and roots such as lemon, apple, cranberries and ginger are used individually or in combination to make tea infusions. Linden and chamomile flowers are also infused with tea leaves. Herbal infusions in water and oil are both commonly used as herbal remedies. Chamomile, for example, is a plant known for its ability to help with sleep and chamomile tea is often served with either honey or lemon. Linden or rose teas are often mixed with alcohol and honey to create wonderful spirits.

Photo 3.2 Linden flowers make wonderful tea.

In cooler climates Linden trees grow everywhere, even on Roosevelt Island in New York City. Unfortunately most people have lost their bond with nature and live entirely on the Internet. Instead of picking up linden flowers for free they spend a fortune buying them as dried flowers in pharmacies or as linden tea in expensive supermarkets.

Alcoholic herbal infusions are cold infusions; they are made with alcohol and don't need to be heated. Alcohol softens the skin, breaks the cell structure and draws out oils, fats, proteins, color agents and flavor substances.

Elixir - a clear, sweet-flavored liquid used for medicinal purposes, to be taken orally and intended to cure one's ills. Just enough alcohol is applied to completely dissolve the main ingredient and produce a clear solution. Vodka can be used for making elixirs.

Polish Infusions

Poland has a long history of creating infusions. A good explanation is the abundance of fruit, nuts and berries that grow everywhere. Add to the fact the great fondness the Poles show towards drinking and there you have it, infusions of all types abound everywhere in Poland.

Until the XVI century the alcoholic beverage that was commonly consumed in Poland was beer. It wasn't just a beverage, it was also consumed as a soup. It was a high caloric food, that due to its high alcoholic content kept surprisingly well. Honey wines were always popular in Poland as grapes did not grow well there.

The drinking habits of a lot of countries changed in the XVIII century when the process of making alcohol from potatoes and grains like barley, wheat and rye was perfected. This combined with the technology of producing inexpensive sugar from sugar beets established the

Photo 3.3 Sour cherry trees on Polish street.

industry for making vodka and other spirits that continues to prosper in Poland. Poor folk drank plain vodka crudely distilled from rye, known as okowita. The more affluent used okowita for making infusions. Those original extracts contained 25-75% alcohol, 30-40% being the average. These were patiently produced drinks as the production time was usually between 3 months to 3 years. The containers were stored in root cellars, sometimes covered only with soil. Later, infusions were stored in large glass containers which did not color them the way oak does. After being poured off into bottles, infusions were submitted to a 6 month aging process, and then came the long awaited moment of tasting. Needless to say, this was an occasion for a huge celebration.

The recipes varied and were closely guarded, becoming secrets of the house. In rich homes there was a dedicated storage room, an "apteka" (pharmacy), where different types of tinctures were stored and guarded. In smaller ones there was at least a large cabinet "apteczka" (little pharmacy) which contained all alcohol based medicaments. The lady of the house was the keeper and the doctor. Those storages were equipped with a multitude of remedies. Stored items included drinks for upset stomach, extracts functioning as anti-venom, herbs and spices for treating wounds, cosmetics, soaps, waxes, bear, fox, raccoon and wolf fat, vinegars, drinks protecting against ghosts, bad dreams and spirits, and even love potions. Common items were kept as well: garlic, dry mushrooms, vinegars, saffron, vanilla, cinnamon, cardamom, nutmeg, allspice, pepper and others. It was a combination of science and witchcraft, where alcoholic tinctures, snake oil and infusions, played an equal and important role.

When sugar became available, infusions became sweeter and liqueurs were introduced. In rich households, during an important occasion, different types of infusions were served with each dish, similar to different wines which are served during the course of a meal. Hunters always took infusions or the stronger Lithuanian honey spirits on overnight hunting expeditions where the drink provided warmth, and greater imagination for story telling. At the same time, women who were waiting for their loved ones were sipping infusions with cakes and coffee. The general consensus became that the world could not function without infusions. It was believed to be a drink that sparked the imagination of the drinker, as well as possessing medicinal values.

Infusions were well known in most European countries, not just in Poland. In Russia, Lithuania, Ukraine and Germany, infusions were regularly consumed. The history of alcoholic drinks in those countries is similar to that of Poland. Originally people drank a lot of beer, fermented honey mixed with juice with hundreds of different types of infusions. Infusions were made from herbs and fruits and mixed with alcohol that was obtained from distilling honey. Keep in mind that centuries ago cane sugar was unheard of and the technology of making sugar from sugar beets was not yet invented. Honey was the universal sweetener. Distillation was already popular, but was mainly reserved for making medicinal drinks. Wine was popular in countries with sunny and warm climates such as Italy, Greece, Spain, Bulgaria and Hungary.

Fruit infusions were made from fruits and herbs by covering them with alcohol. Those original infusions contained only 20-30% of alcohol and could be considered alcoholic extracts. As the distillation process became universally known and the technology permitted making alcohol from grains and potatoes, fruit infusions became more popular and stronger.

Lithuanian Honeys

Lithuanian honeys deserve special mention as they were such wonderful drinks. The best translation would be an alcohol enriched honey wine. Fresh or dry fruits, herbs and aromatic spices were added, and those were mixed with honey and alcohol. Then, they matured for a long time in oak barrels. The Lithuanian honeys contained 50-75% (100 - 150 proof) of alcohol so they were rather potent drinks. Lithuanian honeys were sometimes ignited before serving. While the ignition created a spectacle, the main reason for the ignition was to release alcohol vapors which made the drink taste better, especially in the cold season. It was also proof of the drink's quality and potency, as the weak versions did not inflame.

Flavored Vodkas and Infusions – The Difference

There is not much difference between fruit flavored vodkas and infusions, except the fact that vodkas are finished off to contain 40% alcohol. Flavored vodkas and infusions are made by mixing alcohol, fruit juices, sugar and flavorings together. The composition of infusions is not as precise as that of vodka or liqueur. In traditionally made home infusions all ingredients are placed in a glass jar and left to macerate. Besides shaking the jar or stirring fruit, there is not much work required for the first 4 weeks. This also means that we have to wait quite a while until the infusion is ready to be served.

On the other hand vodka can be drunk the next day. Making an infusion can be considered the first part of the vodka making process. Such infusions are made with fruit and alcohol only, they are filtered and bottled for future use. Sugar is not added as it will prevent using the infusion for making dry vodka. Using this line of reasoning we can see there are two types of infusions:

Alcohol and fruit (or fruit juice) infusion. Such infusions become a raw material for future use. When it has been filtered and becomes clear, we can easily estimate its alcohol strength. It can be added to dry vodkas, sweet vodkas or liqueurs. Herbal infusions fit into this category as well. Having a selection of ready to use popular aromatic extracts/infusions such as vanilla, nutmeg, cinnamon, cloves, star anise, lemon skins and orange skins greatly simplifies the work and makes it possible to make a new spirit in a matter of minutes.

Alcohol, fruit and sugar infusion. Such infusions are ready to drink products, but their usefulness as an ingredient for making other spirits is severely restricted. It can be called fruit vodka and have a wonderful taste, but it is hard to calculate what really sits inside of it. The alcohol that was added, how much sugar was added, and the amount of juice that was released by the fruit is anybody's guess. It is hard to estimate its alcohol content. We can't use a sweet cherry infusion if we want to produce dry cherry vodka.

There is a difference between *distilled* natural fruit vodkas, and spirits and infusions. The main difference is infusions are made by pouring alcohol over raw materials such as fruit, herbs, spices, and sugar. This alcohol has already been distilled in a commercial brewery, the tax has been paid and the government does not care whether you give it to your friend, add it to your lemon tea or make a flavored drink. You can use pure 96% alcohol (192 proof), 75% alcohol (150 proof), 40% (80 proof) vodka or any alcoholic drink like rum or brandy to make your own drinks.

On the other hand, plain vodka, pure alcohol, rum, brandy, and whiskey are spirits made from the fermented must that is distilled in licensed factories. In addition to plain vodkas, there are commercially manufactured flavored vodkas that are made similarly to home infusions.

Alcohol is diluted with flavor essence and water and fruit flavored vodka is produced. The tax is levied on the bottle before it leaves the plant for distribution. At home, you can make wine or beer (no distillation is needed), but it is illegal to distill a drop of alcoholic spirit. *This does not mean that one cannot own distillation equipment. You can distill your own water or herbal extracts, as long as you don't produce alcohol.*

The taste, smell, clarity, and color are all qualities that make infusion superior to plain vodka. One drinks infusion for pleasure, plain vodka is usually taken just to get drunk. Even when vodka is mixed with orange juice, soda, or made into a cocktail, it does not even come close to the beauty, flavor and aroma of a properly made home infusion. In addition to containing all the attributes of vodka, which is just a mixture of alcohol with water, infusions deliver a subtle flavor of fruits, herbs and aromatic spices. Honey is often added and different infusions are mixed together for an even more striking effect. This can be compared to sherry wine, which is a mixture of different wines. Moreover, with the careful selection of fruits and ingredients, infusions can be produced in a variety of colors and strengths. They can be dry, semi-dry, sweet, weak, or strong.

Pouring vodka over fruits, as some books advocate, and drinking it 3-4 days later has little to do with the art of preparing infusions. Such quickly produced drinks are no different than plain vodka that is mixed with fruit juice. The result is a cloudy mixture that just kicks your head. Infusions or fruit vodkas will taste great, that we can take for granted. However, they still have to look pretty and be presentable. Infusions are judged by a panel of experts, similar to a wine contest; they are evaluated by clarity, aroma, taste and flavor. Making top quality infusions is an art form that takes knowledge, time and patience.

Photo 3.4 Home made vodkas and infusions.

Ratafias

From Wikepedia: *"Ratafia is a liqueur or cordial flavored with lemon peel, herbs in various amount typically combined with sugar."*

Ratafia infusions have been popular in Poland for centuries. What separates them from other fruit infusions is that ratafia is meant to be a combination of at least two different fruits, sometimes as many as a dozen. Homemade ratafias were made according to a certain ritual:

1. A large container was used for making ratafia. From the beginning of the season, every new fruit that matured was added into the holding jar. Fruit was washed, cut into smaller parts (apricots, apples, pears), placed in a jar, scattered with sugar and covered with 95% alcohol. Strawberries would be the first ones in the season to go into the jar.

2. Any new fruit that would be ready was added according to the above procedure. About 700 g sugar and 750 ml 95% alcohol was added per 1 kg of fruit. If an insufficient amount of juice was released, a small amount of water was added. Keep in mind that in the past there were no supermarkets and people had to wait for trees to supply the fruits.

3. The procedure continued until the end of the season (almost a year), then the infusion was siphoned, filtered, bottled and stored in the root cellar.

4. And when the snow appeared, ratafia was ready.

Photo 3.5 Ratafia infusion.

Making Infusions

Let's start with the Polish definition of alcoholic infusions known as "nalewka" (pronounced nalevka): *nalewka is an alcoholic drink that is made by pouring alcohol over fresh or dry fruits in such a proportion that the finished product contains about 40% alcohol.* This statement largely restricts the usefulness of 40% vodka for making infusions as it will be further diluted with fruit juices and the resulting product will have the potency of fruit wine. If you want to drink wine, make it the right way by fermenting fruit and there are hundreds of books on the subject. And why do we start with the Polish definition of infusion? Well, they have been making infusions for hundreds of years, so they must be doing it right by now.

How Alcohol Reacts with Fruit

The purpose of adding *strong alcohol* to fruit is not to get people drunk as fast as possible, but to *extract the maximum amount of flavor and aromatic substances the fruit cells contain.* The fresh fruit does not willingly release those substances unless its structure gets damaged. Protoplasm is the living contents of a cell that is surrounded by a plasma membrane. Pectins are like the skeleton and together with the skin they hold everything together. When fruit is covered with alcohol, the solid cell becomes a gel, the membrane becomes softer and it allows two way traffic known as osmosis:

- Alcohol is moving towards the inside of the cell.

- The flavor and aroma substances which are present in juice and cells are moving outside where they become an important part of the newly forming solution.

The main reason that the fruit cells die and allow this exchange is the *loss of water which is removed by alcohol.* Pour a tiny amount of pure alcohol on your hand and you will get an immediate sensation of cold. This is due to an immediate evaporation of moisture from the skin that alcohol removes. It is clear that a strong 95% alcohol will be more effective than a diluted one like 40% vodka. However, pure alcohol is so strong that *it may preserve the fruit instead of extracting its flavor components.* Strong alcohol (85-90%) may only be added to fruit that contains a significant amount of water. Studying old recipes you will notice that 1 liter of 95% alcohol was usually added to 1 kg of fruit. However, about 250 ml of water was also added and that lowered the alcohol strength to 76%. It is generally acceptable that the finished infusion should contain about 50-60% alcohol. Keep in mind that this number will still go down when the syrup and other ingredients are added.

Someone might ask why vodka isn't the best choice for making infusions. Well, *strong 60-80% alcohols* break down the cell structure of fruits, nuts, or herbs very effectively, *fully extracting* flavor components.

Weak alcohols, 40% vodka strength or less, face two problems:

A. Lower quality of infusion due to a weaker flavor extraction.

B. Infusion becomes a weak alcoholic spirit. When alcohol is added to macerated fruit, it becomes diluted with juices and the solution becomes weaker. Adding 40% vodka may result in a drink of 20% alcohol or less, and here we are encroaching on wine territory. Traditional infusions are drinks that should taste wonderful, yet still contain 30-40% alcohol. For those who like softer drinks it is advisable to use strong alcohol (60-70%) to fully extract the flavor substances and then add more water to decrease the strength of the solution. The truth is that many commercially made Polish infusions are very weak. Whether they are made in such a way to lower the cost of alcohol or whether the consumer prefers them that way, I cannot say. However, infusions made in Lithuania or Ukraine still follow the original recipes and contain between 35-40% alcohol.

The process of making infusions does not employ the fermentation step, an infusion is a tincture; alcohol removes flavor and aroma from the fruit and preserves it in a bottle. This opens the door to the huge number of drinks a creative person can make at home and the process is both simple and enjoyable. However, a great deal of patience and attention to detail is needed, as quality infusions need time to mature.

The infusion making process consists of the following steps:

• Material selection (fruits, herbs) and preparation.

• Maceration with alcohol.

• Filtering.

• Aging.

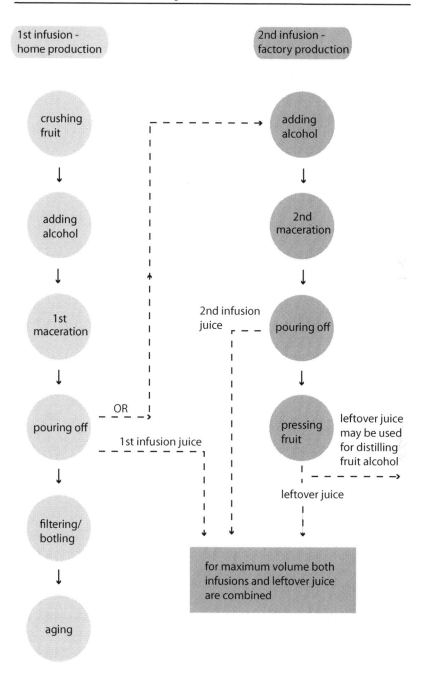

Fig. 3.1 Making infusions.

Maceration is the crucial part of the process when alcohol starts working on a fruit. The complete maceration, at least as employed by commercial producers, consists of two parts:

1. The first infusion.
2. The second infusion.

Both steps are usually employed. However, the infusion can end after the first step. For example, when making vanilla infusion, *the second step is added for purely economic reasons*, specifically to fully extract the ingredients and alcohol that is leftover from the first immersion. Needless to say commercial producers employ two steps to maximize profits.

1. The first infusion produces the highest quality clear juice. The basic steps:

A. *Fruit preparation.* Weighing and washing fruit. Washing fruit also removes some of the natural bacteria that usually reside on the surface. Soft fruit like raspberries are not washed to prevent the loss of juice. They may be showered but not agitated.

B. *Fruit breaking.* The fruit is cut, smashed or holed to facilitate juice release.

C. *Maceration with alcohol.* Fresh fruit must be fully covered with 70-80% alcohol. A typical proportion is between 1–1.5 liter of 70% alcohol to 1 kg of fruit.

The juicier the fruit, the stronger alcohol can be selected.

Dry fruits such as plums, juniper, rowan, and citrus fruit skins contain a little water and are covered with 50-60% alcohol. Glass jars should be 2/3 filled and must be closed tight to prevent alcohol evaporation.

The mixture is usually left for 2-3 weeks and should be stirred every second day. Shaking the jar is even better. An occasional exposure to air creates no problem as no fermentation takes place. Natural yeasts are not able to withstand such concentrations of alcohol so they don't develop. Jars with macerating fruit may be kept in a warm daylight area, but herb infusions should be macerated in a dark and cool place. There isn't any universal macerating time and the process can last from a few days to a few months, depending on the type of fruit and the strength of alcohol.

>   D. *Pouring off.* The juice is siphoned off, carefully poured away or filtered through a cheese cloth. The alcohol strength of the obtained liquid depends on the water content of the fruit and the strength and the amount of alcohol added. For example, mixing 1 kg of tart cherries with 1 liter of 70% alcohol will result in about 1.5 liter liquid at 45% alcohol strength. The resulting infusion should contain 40-45% alcohol.

2. The second infusion is simply repeating the procedure using materials that remain from the first immersion. The fruit pumice still contains much alcohol from the first run, but fewer substances and juices that can be extracted. Thus, the second infusion may be performed with less (0.7 – 1 liter/per kg fruit) and weaker 40-50% alcohol, and 40% vodka fits into this range. The time for the second extraction should be about 3 weeks, supported by frequent stirring. The liquid is siphoned or filtered, but the mixture is left by itself to drain. Forceful squeezing will result in a cloudy liquid, especially noticeable with pectin rich fruit like apples, currants or raspberries.

The liquid from the second infusion is:

- Added to the liquid from the first infusion. This increases the volume of the infusion, but lowers the overall quality. It is also time and space consuming.

- Treated as a separate infusion.

- Distilled to produce fruit distillate. This procedure is performed by commercial producers.

Note: in commercial operations the leftover must is pressed. The resulting liquid is either added to the first and second infusion or distilled and becomes the fruit distillate. Then it is used for making flavored vodka.

An infusion contains the best that the fruit can offer and becomes a great drink in its own right. However, it can be stored as a raw material for making alcoholic spirits later, for example flavored vodka.

Fresh Fruit Infusions

The process of making infusions relies on maceration; the wine making process where the phenolic materials of the fruit (tannins, coloring agents and flavor compounds) are leached from the fruit skins, seeds and stems into the must. All those aromatic oils, color forming substances, minerals, sugars, and proteins are locked inside of the cell and must be extracted. The majority of them will be released in the form of a juice, however, substances responsible for the color are contained in the skin.

The first step in macerating fruit is cutting, pressing or puncturing fruit to increase the surface area. You could extract fruit with a juice extractor, but its clarity will not be as pure as running it through a press. Try to avoid pulverizing pits, seeds or even skins as they contain substances that impart a bitter taste to the product. They also contain pectins which can make the solution cloudy. However, a certain percentage of pits, for example sour cherries or plums are often added as they bring a special and desired flavor.

It is difficult to determine the exact amount of infusion that will be obtained as this depends on the characteristics of the fruit. The same variety of fruit grown in different climate zones will contain a different amount of sugar and juice. Knowing how much juice will be released by a particular fruit will give us a general idea to the alcoholic strength of the infusion. Generally, it may be expected that around 60-80% of juice may be obtained from fresh fruit.

The following table can be used as a point of reference as it reflects the methods used by commercial producers.

Making infusions from 1 kg of fresh fruit						
	First Immersion			Second Immersion		
Material	Alcohol in ml	Alcohol %	Time	Alcohol in ml	Alcohol %	Time
Apple	800	70	3 weeks	600	40	3 weeks
Apricot	800	70	3 weeks	600	40	3 weeks
Blackthorn	1000	70	3 weeks	800	40	3 weeks
Black berries	800	85*	3 weeks	700	40	3 weeks
Black currants	1000	75	4 weeks	650	40	3 weeks
Blue berries	800	80*	3 weeks	700	40	3 weeks
Plums, damson	900	80*	3 weeks	600	40	3 weeks
Raspberries	800	80*	3 weeks	700	40	3 weeks
Rowan	1000	70	3 weeks	800	40	3 weeks
Sour cherries	800	85*	3 weeks	700	40	3 weeks
Strawberries	1000	75	3 weeks	800	40	3 weeks
Walnuts, green	900	60	3 weeks	600	60	3 weeks

* If 95% alcohol is not available, use 75% Everclear® or equivalent.
1 liter = 1000 ml

Citrus Skins

Lemon and orange skins contain a lot of aromatic substances. Orange oil is extracted from the orange peel by cold-pressing and yields 0.3 -0.5 %. Fresh citrus skins are macerated with 75% alcohol for 3-4 days only, as longer maceration introduces a bitter flavor.

Dry Fruit Infusions

Infusions can be made from dry fruit such as raisins, prunes, plums, apricots, figs, juniper, vanilla, rowan, blackthorn, wild rose and others. Dry fruits contain little water but plenty of sugar and concentrated substances that can be extracted. To fully extract ingredients from dry fruit the first and second infusion methods are usually applied. Dry fruits contain almost no juice so the alcohol will not be very diluted. Therefore, a larger amount of weaker alcohol is added. Whereas in the case of fresh fruit we may expect to obtain about 1.5 liters of infusion from 1 kg of fruit, processing 1 kg of dry fruit will usually result in 3-4 liters infusion as more alcohol is added.

The process:

- Soaking dry fruit for 12-24 hours in little water (optional step).
- The first infusion - covering fruit with 3 liters 50% alcohol (per 1 kg of fruit).
- Macerating for 2-3 weeks.
- Siphoning the infusion.
- The second infusion – adding 1.5–1.75 liters 40% alcohol (per 1 kg of fruit).
- Macerating for 2-3 weeks.
- Siphoning the infusion and filtering the must. Cover the container to prevent alcohol evaporation. The first and the second infusions are combined together.

The following table can be used as a point of reference as it reflects the methods used by commercial producers.

Making infusions from 1 kg of dry fruit						
Material	First Immersion			Second Immersion		
	Alcohol in liters	Alcohol %	Time	Alcohol in liters	Alcohol %	Time
Bird cherry (Padus avium)	3	50	4 weeks	1.5	40	3 weeks
Blackthorn	2	50	3 weeks	0.9	40	3 weeks
Figs	5	50	3 weeks	3	40	3 weeks
Prunes	5	50	3 weeks	3	40	3 weeks
Raisins	5	50	3 weeks	3	40	3 weeks
Raspberries	5	50	3 weeks	3'	40	3 weeks
Rowan	8	60	3 weeks	5	40	3 weeks
Vanilla	10	60	3 weeks	7	40	3 weeks

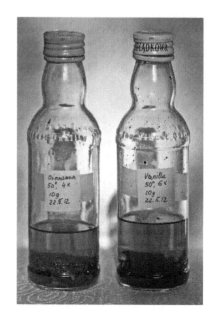

Photo 3.6 Freshly made cinnamon and vanilla infusions. The infusions will be added later as flavoring to other drinks.

Herbal Infusions

Herbal infusions have been made with dry fruits, berries, roots, herbs and spices for hundreds of years. Our early medical science revolved around herbs and spices. They were the first remedies and ointments that the doctor prescribed to a patient, so it is not surprising that they still receive credit. Herbal infusion may be produced from a particular herb or spice, for example cinnamon or cloves, or by mixing different ingredients. For example in 1510 the Benedictine monk, Dom Bernardo Vincelli, created a secret elixir that is still sold today. Bénédictine contains 27 different plants and spices and the recipe is a closely guarded trade secret, known to only three people at any given time.

The flavor compounds from herbs and spices can be extracted by maceration. You can produce an extract from cloves, cinnamon, citrus skins, grass or their blends. The processing method remains basically the same as for dry fruit. The basic steps:

A. Material preparation. The material is cut, ground, smashed to about 1-2 cm (¼-½") particles. Discard the pectin rich white pith of citrus skins.

B. Macerating with alcohol. From 3 to 10 liters of alcohol is applied to 1 kg of herb/spice material. An average amount may be 1 part herb to 5 parts alcohol. Dry materials are macerated from 3-21 days with 40-60% alcohol.

C. Filtering. This is accomplished pouring off the liquid or filtering through a cloth.

Most aromatic herbs and spices owe their aroma to oil compounds they contain. Those oils will dilute easily in strong alcohol, but may come out of solution and become cloudy when the liquid is watered down. On the other hand using weak alcohol will mainly extract substances that dilute easily in water. Such substances contain less aromatic flavors but more acids. The liquid's flavor moves towards the acidic, bitter and sour ends of the scale.

Herbal infusions are manufactured by four methods:

1. Cold extraction.
2. Hot extraction.
3. Percolation.
4. Distillation.

Larger materials, such as cinnamon tree bark or whole nutmeg are usually broken down to 1-2 cm size. Long grass, for example bison grass, is cut to 10 cm length. Leaves such as tea or rose petals may be left intact. The process follows the same steps for making infusions. Material is covered with alcohol and the container is closed tight. The choice of alcohol follows the general guidelines and is related to the amount of water the material contains.

1. Cold extraction

General Guidelines for Making Herbal Infusions			
Material	Alcohol Strength	Time	Notes
Fresh citrus skins	75-80% Single immersion only	3-4 days	Longer times introduce bitterness even if the white pith has been removed.
Dry herbs, dry citrus skins	50% Single immersion	2-3 weeks	Follow the usual standard procedure, see dry fruit immersion. Stir once a day.
	40% Double immersion	2-3 weeks	Follow with double infusion if you want to maximize the amount of infusion, especially when expensive spice like vanilla is used. Then combine infusions together.
3-10 times more alcohol is added in relation to the weight of material e.g. 3-10 liter per 1 kg material.			

It should be noted that pure alcohol dissolves oil but not water so the alcohol strength will influence the type of components the herb will release best:

- High strength alcohol - aromatic oils, fats, resins.

- Low strength alcohol - colorants, bitter compounds, acids, sugars.

Photo 3.7 Star anise infusion.

Pure alcohol may extract and dissolve oils which may come out from the solution when the infusion is later diluted. This may create cloudiness which is not easy to filter. Such an occurrence will be alarming for commercial producers, but not for hobbyists. To summarize, manipulating alcohol strength provides a certain degree of control over the quality of an herbal infusion.

Dry herbs and spices absorb up to 40% of alcohol. To obtain 200 ml of infusion from 20 g of dry herbs we have to add 325 ml of 50% alcohol. Herbs and spices are costlier than fruit, so

it is recommended to go with the second immersion method. Add 200 ml for the first immersion, siphon the infusion out, and then add the remaining 125 ml of alcohol. Siphon out and combine both infusions. They should amount to 200 ml total. As 20 g of herbs were used, 1 g corresponds to 10 ml of infusion. Store in a dark glass jar.

2. Hot extraction. The advantage of this method is that it shortens the time of osmosis or diffusion which takes place at a faster rate at higher temperatures. Because alcohol evaporation may create losses and safety hazards, this methods requires expensive professional equipment. The process takes place at 50-60° C, and 40-60% alcohol is added at 2-5 times the weight of material e.g. 2-5 liter of alcohol per 1 kg material. This is a one stage immersion process lasting from 4-12 hours.

After the infusion is cooled it is bottled. As mentioned, the advantage is saving time and storage space that would otherwise be needed for storing containers.

3. Percolation. This is the same process that we used before for brewing coffee in coffee percolators, but no heating is involved. The difference is in the design: the percolator must release the infusion from the bottom of the container so the fresh alcohol can enter from above and slowly move through the fruit. Of course, the percolator must be covered tight to eliminate alcohol evaporation. The method works well when materials are diced to the same particle size (but not powdered). The same strength and amount of alcohol is used as in the hot extraction method and the process is completed in 1-3 days.

4. Distillation. This is a very vast subject, it is illegal to distill alcohol at home, and we don't cover it here. The process starts like making regular infusion; the fruit is covered with alcohol, left for some time, enriched with alcohol to 45% then the infusion is distilled.

There is another interesting way of producing strong tinctures which relies on an ingenious method of alcohol evaporation. About ¼ of a glass jar is filled with strong alcohol, preferably with 95% alcohol (or 75%) and a cheese cloth bag filled with fruit is placed on top. The bag hangs above the alcohol and its ends hang over the top of the jar. The jar must be closed tight to prevent alcohol vapors from escaping. Alcohol vapors will react with fruit breaking its cell structure and the fruit will start releasing its juice. It should be noted that the liquid level will increase by an inch or so, depending on the shape of the container.

After 3 weeks a wonderful, dry but strong drink is obtained. Then it can be finished off by adding honey, juice, sugar or water. It is recommended to puncture the skin of the fruit (no need for raspberries) to facilitate the release of juice. As explained earlier, sugar does not dissolve well in pure 95% alcohol, so it is possible to discover a crystal or two. They can be dissolved in a small amount of water and added to the tincture.

Filtering

Filtering is the step that gives the final touch to your master piece. It makes it clear and aesthetically pleasing.

Photo 3.8 Filtering in progress.

Infusions if left undisturbed, should clarify themselves with bigger particles of fruit settling down on the bottom. Then siphoning the liquid with a plastic wine tube will do the trick. The sediment can

also be filtered by running it through a filter. It is a very slow process and the container should be well covered in order to protect alcohol from evaporating. Fruits that contain a lot of pectin, like lemons, have a tendency to produce cloudy liquids.

Most people use a funnel that is lined with a paper towel, coffee filter, medical gauze, cheese cloth or even make up removing pads.

Photo 3.9 Funnel and gauze.

Using one funnel can be a slow and tedious operation which can be improved by simply using more funnels. Pour the infusion through a strainer into each filter and the operation will be faster.

Paper towels filter well and they are disposable which makes them easy to use. Nylon cheese cloth is a great filter material that is easy to wash.

Certain fruits such as sour cherries or kiwi produce clear juices while others like lemon or plums appear cloudier.

Photo 3.10 Using more filters speeds up filtering.

Photo 3.11 Kiwi fruit seems to look cloudy but it produces an exceptionally clear juice.

Photo 3.12 Left glass - freshly strained kiwi infusion (fruit and alcohol, no sugar). Middle glass - the same infusion the next day. Note the sediment on the bottom. Right glass - freshly strained juice was filtered through a paper towel. It is crystal clear.

Photo 3.13 Left glass - honey vodka was strained and filtered twice through paper towel. It is still somewhat cloudy. Right glass - the same vodka was strained, left to rest for two days, then siphoned leaving sediment behind. It is crystal clear even with 30% sugar present.

Photo 3.14 Pharmacist infusion is difficult to filter. It is made by combining fresh lemons, regular milk and strong alcohol. This mixture creates a cheese like substance on the bottom and clear liquid on top. Siphon the clear liquid away and filter the rest. Then filter again.

Photo 3.15 Filtered pharmacist infusion.

You can use any kind of filtering system, but the following method works very well:

1. Strain the infusion through a fine sieve. You can use the fruit for making the second infusion.

Photo 3.16 Straining ratafia (multi fruit infusion).

2. Pour the infusion into a tall bottle. Let the infusion sit for one or two days. All bigger particles will sink to the bottom and a clear liquid will form on top.

Photo 3.17 Small strainer fits right into the funnel.

3. Siphon the clear liquid away.

It is difficult to siphon a small amount of infusion, for example 500 ml, that remains in a large jar. In such cases it is recommended to use a tall but small diameter container.

Photo 3.18 Both containers hold an equal amount of infusion (500 ml) and the same amount of sediment.

Photo 3.19 On the left, in the wide diameter jar, the sediment layer is very small and will be easily disturbed. In the narrow diameter but tall flask, the sediment layer is high and all clear liquid will be easily siphoned.

Infusions which are made with fruit and alcohol only tend to filter easily. When a significant amount of sugar is present, filtering becomes hard. A simplified "racking" process works faster and better. Racking is the term used for filtering wine. Fermented wine, even if it was made from fresh juice, contains little parts of fruit and dead yeast. All those particles sink to the bottom creating a layer of sediment. The clear wine is siphoned away to another container and left again for a month. Then it is siphoned again. At the end only clear wine remains.

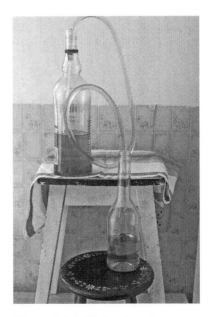

Photo 3.20 Siphoning in progress.

Don't disturb a strained infusion before filtering. Try to siphon the clear liquid first, and run the rest through the filter. Combine liquids together and filter again.

Ratafia infusions are made in larger quantities and to filter 10-20 liters of freshly made infusion will take too long using small equipment. Use a big filtering bag and a suitable vessel.

Strain the liquid first through a strainer, then place the leftover fruit in a big filter bag and let it drip over night.

Photo 3.21 Straining ratafia.

Photo 3.22 Filtering the leftover fruit.

Then combine liquids together and filter again. You don't need much space or specialized equipment to produce 10 liters of ratafia. What's important is the proper organization and workflow.

Gelling Agents

There are gelling agents on the market which help to clarify wines. They can be used for infusions as well. A typical wine fermenting glass carboy holds 20 liters so the extra cost and savings in time is well justified. Home infusions are made on a much smaller scale and a simple filtering system is all that is needed.

Blending

This is the exciting tasting step where you find out how well your product has turned out. You can add more water to make it softer or add more alcohol for the opposite result. You may sweeten it up, or mix a few types of infusions together. You can add food coloring for a better visual effect. By all means do whatever pleases you, after all you will drink it. The process, however, is not finished yet and one more step remains.

Aging/Storing

The quality of infusions improve with time as they mature and mellow. Six months is usually plenty. They are best stored in dark glass bottles, and in cool, dark places they will last for years. When the infusion is clear it is ready to be bottled. Dark glass is suitable and used wine jars with twisted tops work well. White glass bottles without twisted tops are fine, just be sure to get fresh corks and keep the bottles in a dark room or cellar. Fruit infusions should age for 1-6 months or even longer. The only exceptions are milk based infusions that should be stored in a refrigerator and consumed within a month or two. During the aging process infusions mellow, the individual flavors and aromas blend in together and a superior quality drink is obtained.

Home Production

Traditional home production calls for adding sugar, water, and alcohol to fruit at the same time. After 3 weeks of maceration time, the infusion is siphoned off and left to age for a few months. The longer the better; there is no risk of spoiling as alcohol preserves infusion. Then it is re-checked for clarity, carefully siphoned and poured into bottles. In a worst case scenario it may have to be filtered before bottling. Homemade infusions usually employ the first immersion method to save time and space. If space is of little concern and a large amount of fruit is available, much more infusion will be produced when the second immersion is employed.

Home Made Infusions

- First infusion is made without sugar.
- Sugar and alcohol are added to the fruit (the second infusion).
- Both infusions are then combined.

After the first or the second infusion ends there is still a certain amount of juice and alcohol that remains in the fruit. It can be filtered through a cheese cloth or gauze. Don't squeeze the mash; let gravity take its course.

The best of the fruit is removed by the first infusion and combining both infusions will create a lower quality product. It is advisable to keep both batches separately as two distinct products. A smart solution is to add essential oil at 0.1 g per 10 liters to the second infusion to enhance its flavor.

Often the first infusion is made with alcohol only. After macerating, the infusion is filtered and kept for future use. However, sugar and some alcohol is added to fruit leftovers and left to macerate again. Then it is filtered and bottled as a separate infusion.

Almost all traditional recipes are made in this manner:

- Fruit preparation.
- Adding sugar.
- Adding alcohol.
- Macerating.
- Pouring off/filtering.
- Aging.

This is a fine method and a great infusion can be produced. The factory model offers more benefits:

- Infusion can be stored as a raw material. Sugar will be added when the composition of the infusion is determined.
- It is easier to calculate the infusion's alcoholic strength and its sugar content.
- Filtering is easier as the infusion is generally thinner.

Commercial producers perform macerating without sugar. Infusion becomes a ready to use material, one of many components of a flavored spirit that will be made. Sugar or syrup is added when the final blending takes place.

The maximum time for creating infusions is 4-6 weeks, otherwise the quality becomes lower. Usually, 3-4 weeks is all that is needed.

Extracts

Extracts can be thought of as weaker essential oils that can add extra flavor to an infusion. There are hundreds of available extracts to choose from. Simple flavoring infusions/extracts can be made at home.

Photo 3.23 VSOP infusion extracts. All it takes is to mix 50 ml of the extract with 1 liter of plain vodka, and then let it age for one day.

Photo 3.24 A good collection of infusions and extracts allows creating new spirits instantaneously.

Chapter 4

All About Vodka

History

In Poland, vodka has been produced since the early Middle Ages. The word "vodka" was first written in 1405 in Akta Grodzkie, the court documents from the Palatinate of Sandomierz in Poland. The definition applied to early alcoholic tinctures that were prescribed for medicinal and aesthetic purposes.

The first written use of the word vodka in an official Russian document in its modern meaning is dated via the decree of Empress Elizabeth in June 8, 1751, which regulated the ownership of vodka distilleries. Alcoholic spirits were produced in Russia much earlier than 1751. At the beginning of the XVI century, vodka became synonymous with the Polish word "gorzalka" which means strong alcoholic drink and both words are commonly used. Then the word found its way to Russia. The dispute about which country invented the drink continues even today, the pronunciation and the spelling is almost identical; Polish "wodka" and Russian "vodka" describe something that is derived from water, and this is exactly what the drink is; alcohol diluted with water.

Starting in the XV century, the first vodkas, also called wodka, okowita or gorzalka became a popular alcohol drink mainly among peasants. In the XVI century nobility started to drink the spirit as well and that led to a universal acceptance of the drink. The consumption jumped so high the manufacturing and selling of vodka was taxed. Poland started to supply vodka to neighboring countries. Russian merchants exchanged furs and skins for vodka. Vodka was also exported to Czechoslovakia and Hungary. As the word spread other countries such as Germany, England and France started to appreciate the drink. The new industry in Poland took off and soon spirits were produced in many cities: Warsaw, Lwow, Gdansk, Gniezno and Poznan.

The ongoing discussions of who invented the word 'vodka' is trivial as Poland was the first country that produced the spirit on a large scale. The city of Krakow was manufacturing and exporting vodka in 1550. There were 49 large distillation machines in 1580 in Poznan. Those centers were producing different types of vodka and liqueurs. One of the biggest centers was Gdansk (Danzig) where a total of 680 breweries operated non-stop. In 1598 Gdansk started the production of outstanding liqueurs that were exported to Germany, Holland, France and England. The best known liqueur was Goldwasser (Gold Water) which is still popular today.

The general acceptance of the spirit led to increased consumption in Poland and in other countries. In the XVII century the average consumption was 5 liters of vodka per person. The first industrial distillery was opened in 1782 in Lwów by J. A. Baczewski and his products are still available today. He was soon followed by Jakub Haberfeld, who in 1804 established a factory in Oswiecim, and by Hartwig Kantorowicz, who started producing Wyborowa in 1823 at Poznan. In 1925 the production of vodkas was monopolized by the government. After World War II, all vodka distilleries were taken over by Poland's communist government.

When WWII ended in 1945, Poland along with other countries was taken over by the Stalin regime which created a new political system. The currencies of those countries were not recognized by the West and they were faced with enormous difficulties in obtaining hard currency (dollar) in order to purchase machines and tools from the West for rebuilding their economy. One of the main dollar earners became Polish vodka which was made by the state run Polmos company. Polmos produced outstanding vodkas and some of them such as Wyborowa, Luksusowa, Zytnia, Zubrowka and Spirytus (95% alcohol) flooded the U.S. market.

Vodka brands like Absolut, Finlandia, and Bols were not common yet. Polish vodkas dominated the market. Russians followed with Stolichnaya and Americans started to produce Smirnoff. All those vodkas were plain spirits with a neutral taste and led themselves perfectly for making mixed drinks. Remember James Bond's favorite drink: "vodka on the rocks, shaken but not stirred."

Between 1962 and 1990 Polish Wyborowa has participated in 29 World Competitions and has won 29 medals, 22 of which were gold. After the victory of the Solidarity movement, all distilleries were privatized, leading to an explosion of brands. In the 1990's Wyborowa was bought by French Pernod Ricard but was little promoted. In 2002 roku Wyborowa won the International High Quality Trophy from Monde Selection and it has won the gold medal for three consecutive years in the Monde Selection competitions. It has been probably the best vodka ever and it is a pity it has not been better marketed or diversified into flavored varieties sooner.

Vodka Types

There are two types of vodkas:

- Plain vodkas
- Flavored vodkas

Plain vodkas are made from 95% alcohol. Superior quality types like "Wyborowa" are made from 96.5% alcohol. Plain vodka is the simplest, the most unsophisticated alcoholic beverage of them all, consisting of essentially nothing else than a mixture of 40% ethanol (C_2H_5OH) and 60% water (H_2O). Of course, there may be small amounts of impurities in the brew, but they are truly minute. Because it has no taste, the explanation that someone likes the taste of it makes little sense. What we really like is that it kicks our head. When we say this vodka tastes good we really mean that the vodka has a clean, smooth, *neutral* taste. And having a neutral taste means no taste at all. It is relatively easy to recognize a good quality spirit. If you drink plain vodka and your body demands a chaser you have a regular vodka type. This is why such vodkas need to be mixed with sodas or orange juice, because they leave an unpleasant taste. This is of course due to the quality of alcohol that was used to make it. You can drink top quality plain vodka without shaking and you do not need a chaser. There is no unpleasant feeling in the mouth. Using 95% alcohol for making vodka is not a guarantee of a top quality product. If not enough *head (first 3-4% of distillate)* was removed, or distillation continued too long and too much *tail (last 3-5% of distillate)* remained in the distillate, the quality of *heart (main, pure alcohol)* will be poor even if its strength remains at 95-96% level.

Photo 4.1 Distiller on the right, filter on the left. *Photo courtesy VSOP www.vsop.com.pl*

The popularity of vodka can be attributed to two factors:

- It has a neutral taste and color so it becomes a base for many other mixed drinks.

- It is very easy to make – it is made by diluting pure alcohol.

Flavored Vodkas

What has become very popular in recent years is flavored vodka. Flavored vodkas are not new, about 100 different types were once produced in Poland. Flavored vodkas and alcohol based fruit drinks were always popular in Poland, Russia or Germany. However, Russians deserve the credit for recognizing the opportunity and bringing flavored Stolichnayas to the American market. The trend was immediately copied by other manufacturers and flavored vodkas became a hit. Today the following brands produce the majority of flavored vodkas: Stolichnaya – Russian, Finlandia – Finland, Absolut – Sweden. In the USA vodka outsells other spirits like brandy, cognac, gin or whisky. For many years vodka was just pure alcohol 95-96% that has been watered down to 40% (80 proof) strength.

This resulted in a clear spirit of a neutral taste, providing the alcohol was of a good quality. This definition has recently been expanded as there are dozens of lemon, orange, plumb and raspberry flavored vodkas which entered the market. They share the common denominator – they are all 40% (80-proof) strong. They start to resemble Polish and Lithuanian infusions which have been always produced in Polish and Lithuanian households.

As the name implies flavored vodkas are very different. *They are supposed to be different* from plain vodkas. This type of vodka can easily be made at home. Making any kind of vodka requires alcohol, so it is crucial that we understand its properties. Alcohol is mixed with water to produce plain dry vodkas and is added to fruit juices or infusions to make fruit vodkas. You can also make a fruit flavored vodka from a fruit distillate. Alcohol distillates can be produced from fruits, grains, potatoes, molasses or flavored alcohol infusions.

Depending on the amount of sugar alcoholic beverages may be classified as:

- Dry – up to 50 g (5%) of sugar per 1 liter of vodka. There are very few types of vodka without any added sugar at all. Adding as little as one teaspoon/liter (0.04%) of sugar smoothens the taste of regular vodka.
- Semi-dry - 51-120 g/l (5-12%).
- Semi-sweet - 121-220 g/l (12-22%).
- Sweet - 221-330 g/l (22-33%).
- Liqueurs - 331 g/l and more (> 33%).
- Crèmes - 400 g/l or more (> 40%).

We do not necessarily have to follow those standards, but they at least provide a reference point. There is a very fine line that separates sweet flavored vodka from a liqueur. You can make both from the same fruit, for example from sour cherries, although the liqueur will usually incorporate more sugar. *What one person calls sweet vodka another might call a liqueur.* The main advantage of creating alcoholic spirits at home is that one is in total control of the process. One does not have to conform to the government's standards and he can choose the strength of his drink, the amount of sugar or the shape of the bottle. One can experiment a lot, or change the composition of his recipe on a whim, something that the factory cannot do. Factories use automated lines to fill the bottles and increasing the amount of sugar or changing the shape of a bottle will disrupt the production routine.

Vodka Production

There are two methods of making vodkas:

1. Distillation.

- Distilling fermented grains or fruits (fermentation is involved). This method is not recommended for a hobbyist as it is illegal in the USA to distill any type of alcohol at home.

- Distilling fruit infusions (no fermentation is involved). This method is also not recommended for a hobbyist as it is illegal in the USA to distill any type of alcohol at home.

2. Mixing.

- Mixing alcohol with infusions, juices, sugar and other ingredients. A commercial plant usually distills its own alcohol for that purpose; a hobbyist will buy alcohol in a store. The manufacturing process is the same for both.

1. Distilling Fermented Fruit, Grains or Alcoholic Infusions.

The first half of the process is similar to making wine. Let us assume that we have made grape wine and we want to distill it. Once it is distilled its name suddenly changes to English brandy, Polish winiak or if it were produced from grapes growing in the town of Cognac, it can be legally called Cognac. Yet it is just distilled white grape wine. Call it grape vodka if you like.

As you can make wine from almost any fruit, a strong flavored spirit can be obtained by distilling the fermented mash. If distillation were proceeding at full strength, the result will be 96.5% alcohol and 3.5% water, *without* any dominant flavor. *All distilled spirits are clear*, they owe their color to:

- Flavoring, for example caramel.

- Maturing in oak barrels (brandy, cognac) where they receive their color from the wood. A simplified method of creating this type of color in home conditions is adding oak wood chips into the spirit.

Distilled spirits that must remain clear will be aged in clay or glass containers. Different fruits will impart a different flavor to the distillates, some of which are listed below:

Grape Brandies	Fruit Brandies	Grain Spirits	Molasses
Brandy, Armagnac, Cognac, Polish Winiak	Apple (Calvados), Plum (Slivovitz), Sour Cherry (Kirsch)	Rye Vodka, American Whiskey, Barley (Scotch Whiskey), Rice (Arak)	Sugar cane (Rum)

Someone might say: yes, but does distillation result in pure alcohol without taste or flavor? Yes, it does but only if you want it to. The reason that pure alcohol has no taste is that we have removed everything we possibly could including substances responsible for flavor. If we control the distillation process in such a way that it produces 60-75% alcohol, the distillate will be composed of alcohol, water, *plus* all those substances that stamp the product with its characteristic taste and flavor. Cognac, which is distilled white grape wine, cannot be made stronger than 72% otherwise it will lose all those flavors that make it what it is. By distilling fermented fruit mash to about 60-75% we obtain a distillate that is used for making flavored vodkas. Such a distillate contains essential oils, flavor substances, fats, proteins, acids and color substances which evaporated together with alcohol and subsequently were cooled down to form a distillate. They contribute to the flavor of the alcoholic spirit. If the same fermented fruit mash were distilled to 95% we would obtain a pure neutral tasting alcohol which is devoid of all those flavor creating compounds. It becomes evident now that all distilled spirits like brandy, whisky, gin, or rum must be distilled to the alcohol strength that will allow flavor compounds to escape with alcohol vapors and become a part of the distillate.

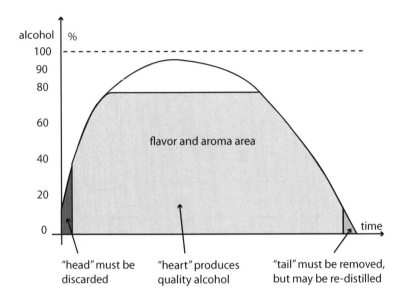

Fig. 4.1 Different ranges of distillation, head, heart, tail, flavor range, pure alcohol.

Most distillates undergo a maturing process for a couple of years for their taste and flavor to mellow. The distillate will lose some strength through alcohol evaporation. Most spirits are kept in oak barrels and these are tight enough to prevent leaks, nevertheless alcohol vapors are still able to get through. They may be 60% strength when submitted for the final tests before bottling. Then they will be diluted with water to 40% and flavored vodkas would be created. In time the distillate which is aged in oak casks acquires a brown color typical to cognac, brandy or whiskey. This should be kept in mind as it will influence the final color of the spirit. A customer would not want to drink brown gin, that is for sure.

Natural Distilled Vodkas

Grape Brandies

Brandy (from brandywine, derived from Dutch brandewijn - "burnt wine") is a spirit produced by *distilling* wine. The wine is heated ("burnt"), vaporized and then cooled becoming brandy. Grape vodkas were originally made in France and were called "eau-de-vie" (vodka from wine). The strength of the distillate is 60-75%, anything stronger will remove too many substances that contribute to the peculiar flavor of brandy or cognac. Then it is aged for 3-5 years and diluted to around 40%. Brandies may be considered a type of flavored fruit vodka as the technology remains basically the same for making other distilled spirits.

Armagnac is a distinctive kind of brandy produced in the Armagnac region in Gascony, southwest France. It is *distilled* from wine usually made from a blend of Armagnac grapes, using column stills rather than the pot stills required in the production of Cognac. The resulting spirit is then aged in oak barrels before release. Armagnac was one of the first areas in France to begin distilling spirits, but the brandies produced have a lower profile than those from Cognac and the overall volume of production is far smaller. In addition they are for the most part made and sold by small producers, whereas Cognac production is dominated by big-name brands.

Armagnac is traditionally *distilled once*, which results in a stronger, more pronounced flavor than that of cognac, where double distillation usually takes place. The distillate is about 52-60% strong. However, long aging in oak barrels softens the taste and causes the development of more complex flavors and a brown color. When the alcohol reaches 40%, the Armagnac is transferred to large glass bottles for storage. From then on the Armagnac does not age or develop further and can be bottled from the next year on.

Cognac, named after the town of Cognac in France, is a certain type of brandy. It is produced in the wine-growing region surrounding the town from which it takes its name. For a distilled brandy to bear the name Cognac, its production methods must meet certain legal requirements. It must be made from specified grapes and the wine must be *twice distilled* in traditional copper pot stills to about 70% alcohol. Then it is aged at least two years in French oak barrels from Limousin or Tronçais oak trees.

Fruit Brandies

Calvados is an *apple brandy* from the French region of Basse-Normandie or Lower Normandy. The fruit is pressed into a juice that is fermented and *distilled*. The best calvados are made in the Pays d'Auge region. Double distillation is carried out in a traditional alembic pot still; the first distillation to 30% alcohol strength, the second distillation to 65-70%. Then it is diluted to about 50% and aged for 2 years in oak casks. Then, if needed, it is diluted to about 42% and bottled.

Slivovitz is a plum brandy, made from *damson plums*, and produced in Slavic regions of Central and Eastern Europe, both commercially as well as by many households. Primary producers are in Serbia, Czech Republic, Slovakia, Poland, Hungary, and Bulgaria. Similar plum brandies are also produced in Germany, Switzerland, France, the United States, and Canada.

Photo 4.2 Damson plum.

The process: plums are drilled but 15-20% kernels are saved as they contain *amygdalin*, the characteristic component of bitter almonds. This peculiar flavor is desired in a plum or sour cherry brandy.

The fruit mash is fermented, then *distilled*:

1st distillation – 25-30%

2nd distillation – 70-75%

Then the slivovitz is aged for 1- 2 years in oak casks. After aging slivovitz is diluted to the required strength, often left at 70% alcohol, which makes it a very strong drink. Sugar is not added to slivovitz.

Kirsch or Kirschwasser is a clear, colorless fruit brandy traditionally made from double *distillation* of morello cherries, a dark-colored cultivar of the sour cherry. The technology follows the process for making slivovitz with one difference: more crushed kernels are added (20-35%), sometimes even all of them. This accounts for the strong cherry-almond flavor of the spirit. The distillate is aged in clay or glass containers in order to preserve its clear color. You may find many Kirsch liqueurs, which are colored and much weaker than brandy.

Grain Vodkas

The best Polish vodkas are made from rye:

- Superior quality dry vodkas – made from 96.5% pure rye alcohol and water, for example Wyborowa Vodka.
- Dry vodkas made from high quality rye alcohol, water and no more than 1.5 g/liter of fruit distillates or infusions. Those vodkas are known as Zytnia Vodkas, *zyto* means rye in Polish. In addition there are many types of vodka that are very slightly flavored with pepper, bison grass, citrus skins and other aromatic substances.

Whiskey

Whiskey is made from fermented grain mash. Different grains are used for different varieties, including barley, malted barley, rye, malted rye, wheat, and corn. Whiskies are usually *distilled* twice to around 63% and aged for at least 2 years in wooden casks, made generally of charred white oak. Most whiskies are sold at or near an alcoholic strength of 40% (80 proof). There are many types of whiskey and they have different processing procedures. The following are the whiskies with the longest tradition: Scotch Whiskey, Irish Whiskey, American Whiskey and Canadian Whiskey. American Bourbon Whiskey is made from grains, but corn must account for at least 51% of the total.

Arrack

From Wikipedia: Arrack, also spelled arak, is a *distilled* alcoholic drink typically produced in South Asia and Southeast Asia, made from either the fermented sap of coconut flowers, sugarcane, grain (e.g. red rice) or fruit, depending upon the country of origin. Java and Sri-Lanka are islands with a long tradition of making this spirit. The clear distillate may be blended, aged in wooden barrels, or repeatedly distilled and filtered depending upon the taste and color objectives of the manufacturer. The basic materials are either rice and sugar molasses or rice and palm wine. The rice is malted, the mash is fermented, distilled and aged. The drink is clear or light yellow, around 60% alcohol strength.

Arrack is not to be confused with arak, an anise-flavored alcoholic beverage traditionally consumed in Eastern Mediterranean and North African countries. In the Middle East and Near East, the term arak is usually used for liquor distilled from grapes and flavored with anise.

Rum

Rum is a distilled alcoholic beverage made from sugarcane by-products such as molasses, or directly from sugarcane juice, by a process of fermentation and distillation. The distillate, a clear liquid, is then usually aged in oak barrels.

There are two types of rum:

- Dark – strong flavor and aroma, darker color, originating in Jamaica.
- Light – Cuba, Puerto Rico. Clear rums exhibit a lighter taste and aroma.

One of the best known producers is Bacardi from Puerto Rico. The factory makes light and medium rums, from 40 to 75%. Then there are many rums which are made in Martinique, Guadeloupe, Guyana, Barbados, Belize, Nicaragua and other islands or countries located in the Caribbean basin area.

This is where most sugar cane plantations have been established. However, rum is also produced in the Canary Islands of Spain, Australia, New Zealand, Fiji, Mexico, Hawaii, the Philippines, India, Mauritius, South Africa, and Canada.

The typical process consists of distilling the fermented sugarcane mash to about 70-75%. Distillation is performed twice and the distillate is usually 70-75% strong. Then it is aged for at least one year. The color of rum is influenced by the type of the aging container; the oak casks will make the rum brown but stainless containers will preserve the clear color of the distillate. Most rums are 40% grade but there are also 55% and 75% stronger ones, for example 75% Bacardi.

Many rums are flavored by the addition of spices and sometimes caramel. Popular spices are cinnamon, rosemary, aniseed, or pepper. Flavored rums are infused with flavors of fruits, such as banana, mango, orange, citrus, coconut, star fruit or lime.

Distilled alcoholic spirits are made with a standard method: fruit preparation, fermentation, distillation to the required alcohol strength which sometimes involves diluting distillate with water and aging. Although those spirits carry their own established names, they may be considered flavored vodkas as flavored vodkas can be a blend of different materials and flavorings.

You must realize by now that distillation is a fairly accomplished process that requires expensive equipment and a lot of space and time. What is even more important, distilling alcohol is illegal in the USA and most countries, so there is no need to go deeper into production details. However, one can buy strong alcohol and create his new combinations or imitate well known products, for example combining rum, brandy, alcohol, sugar and eggs to make a home version of Advocaat.

Distilling Infusions

Generally any fruit infusion can be distilled to make fruit flavored alcohol. The process is similar to making the first infusion method: fruit preparation, adding alcohol and maceration. The maceration process lasts only about 12 hours and the infusion is then distilled.

Gin

Gin is a spirit which derives its predominant flavor from juniper berries (*Juniperus communis*). The name gin is derived from either the French geniĕvre or the Dutch jenever, which both mean "juniper". From its earliest beginnings in the Middle Ages, gin has evolved over the course of a millennium from an herbal medicine to a popular spirit of today. There are a few popular methods for making gin:

- Juniper berries are added into 75-85% alcohol, macerated for 12 hours and distilled.

- Juniper berries are covered with 50-60% alcohol and macerated for 14 days. This is a typical infusion process. Then the infusion is distilled.

- Juniper berries are soaked in water until they release juice. This may be repeated a few times using the juice from the previous maceration to soak new berries. It is possible to obtain 1.2-1.5 liter of juice from 1 kg of berries. Then the juniper juice is fermented for about 2 weeks. Dry juniper berries contain plenty of sugar (20-25%) and will ferment like wine. Then the juniper "wine" is distilled, filtered and aged in clay or glass containers.

Photo 4.3 Dry juniper berries.

2. Making Vodkas by Mixing Method.

Mixing alcohol with infusions, juices, sugar and other ingredients. This is the second method that commercial producers use for making flavored vodkas and other spirits. Here a hobbyist can do anything in his apartment that a brewery does, and the results may be even better. The only difference is the brewery produces its own 95% alcohol and the hobbyist will buy 95% or 75% alcohol from a store. Flavored vodkas are made by mixing pure alcohol with flavor essences, colorings and water in such a proportion that around 40% (80-proof) flavored spirit is obtained.

There is very little difference between infusion and vodka. Vodkas are usually 40% strong; an infusion can be made of any strength. Infusions having an alcohol content below 40% can still be used for vodkas as alcohol can be added to increase the strength. However, it is recommended to make such infusions with fruit and alcohol only. The common practice in traditional recipes is to mix sugar, fruit and alcohol on day one. It will be difficult to calculate the strength and sweetness of vodka if sugar based infusions were mixed together. Another problem is that you cannot produce dry vodka from a sweet infusion and not everybody is fond of sweet spirits.

The process of making flavored vodkas is based on mixing materials such as:

- 95% or 75% alcohol. It may be difficult to purchase 95% alcohol in the USA, but the 75% version is available.
- Infusions.
- Alcohol juices.
- Fresh fruit juices.
- Sugar syrup.
- Essential oils.
- Herbs and spices or their infusions.
- Caramel or colorants.

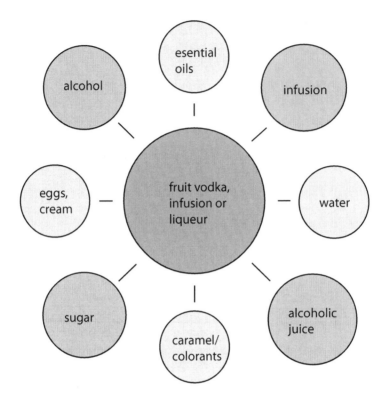

Fig. 4.2 Making flavored vodkas.

Different types of vodka that may be produced at home by the mixing method:

- Plain vodkas - dry vodkas made from a store bought distillate. They may contain some flavoring such as juniper, pepper, bison grass and a very small amount of sugar, usually less than 5 g/l.

- Fruit vodkas - Rowan, Blackthorn (Sloe plum), Juniper, Plum, Green Walnut, Orange, Lemon, Mango, Plum, Cherry, Sour Cherry, Apple, Pear, Peach etc.

- Herbal dry or sweet vodkas - Pepper, Red Pepper, Bison Grass (Zubrowka).

- Herbal bitter vodkas - Magenbitter, Boonekamp, English Bitter, Polish Bitter, Angostura. This type is credited with helping digestion. These are modern versions of traditional tincures and are taken for their medicinal value, usually one or two drinks before the meal.

- Gin - gin can be made by simply flavoring alcohol with juniper berries without involving distillation. The infusion may be enhanced by adding sugar, dry citrus skins or Angelica archangelica root.

Fruit infusions can be classified as fruit vodkas as long as their strength remains around 40%. Many commercially produced dry vodkas such as gin, brandy, and orange vodka require distillation which is illegal outside the industry. Because of that our discussion is limited to making vodkas by the infusion method. The infusion method will produce a wonderful product, however, depending on the fruit selected, the clarity of the spirit may vary.

Dry Vodkas

Dry vodkas are usually made with dry fruit or berries with 60% alcohol. Sugar is added at 1-5%, which is 10-50 g/liter. After maceration, the liquid is strained and the vodka is composed by using infusion, alcohol, sugar syrup, flavorings or other infusions, caramel coloring etc. Then a small amount of water is added to round up the amount to 1 liter.

Bitter Vodkas

Bitter vodkas are very popular in Europe due to the long tradition of making "healing" herbal remedies. One or two shots are taken before a meal to help digestion. Depending on the amount of sugar they may be classified as:

- Dry
- Sweet
- Liqueurs

Sweet Vodkas

Vodkas in this group can be made from any available fruit, contain more sugar and appeal to more customers. Very often they combine a few fruits together and go by the name "ratafia." Adding 5-30% sugar (50-300 g/liter) produces sweet vodkas, but this is of course a loosely defined limit. There is little distinction between sweet vodka and alcoholic fruit infusion, what separates the two is the alcohol strength.

Similarly to wine, the sweeter the vodka the darker its color. It is recommended to add around 0.01% (0.1 g/l) of citric acid to sweet vodkas as this offsets some of the sweetness and smoothens the flavor.

There are two methods for making fruit vodkas:

1. Preparing an infusion of fruit and alcohol. This becomes a material that will be used for final blending of ingredients.
2. Making vodka infusion from fruit, alcohol, sugar and spices. A filtered infusion can be considered a vodka.

1. The first approach offers certain advantages:

You may experiment with a new fruit. There are many fruits such as guava, passion fruit, mango, persimmon, papaya, pineapple, kiwi, loquat, kumquat, tamarind, banana, lychee and others that offer new possibilities but we are not sure of the outcome. If you follow a new recipe and or mix for example kiwi with sugar, spices and other juices you will never know how a pure infusion of kiwi and alcohol tastes or even looks like. But if you mix it with 70% alcohol and macerate for 3 weeks you will discover its sweetness, the color and the clarity. And it will be around 35-40% strong. You may like it the way it is, or you may add a few percent sugar, some water and you have just made 40% vodka. Or you may leave it as a raw base material that you will use later on. Keep in mind that infusions made from fruit and alcohol only are easier to filter. Once sugar has been added it tends to clog the filter's pores and the process is much slower. You can test your new ideas by making a very small amount of infusion.

2. There is nothing wrong with the traditional approach of putting all ingredients in a jar, as long as you are sure that's exactly what you want. If the recipe has been proven before, this is an acceptable method.

Freshly made vodkas need at least two days to mellow as the alcohol has a tendency to stand out in a freshly mixed spirit.

Popular Fruits

Certain fruits have a distinctive flavor and have been favored by hobbyists:

Sour Cherry

Sour cherries make great infusions and vodkas. At the first bite the fruit seems to be tart and sour, but adding sugar transforms it to a different level. It is a favorite of hobbyists all over the world. Regular cherry may seem to taste better and is easier to find, however, it does not compare to the flavor and aroma of sour cherry. The popularity of sour cherries is due to the following factors:

- The fruit produces a lot of juice.
- The juice has a nice reddish color and is very clear.
- The fruit has its own distinct character.
- Sour cherry mixes exceptionally well with other juices and honey. This permits the creation of many fruit vodkas.
- Crushed sour cherry pits provide a unique flavor to the juice.

Cherries and sour cherries prefer cold climates and most American production is localized in the state of Michigan. In North Europe they grow everywhere.

Basic recommendations

Making sour cherry vodka with fresh juice:

- Use matured dark sour cherries.
- Crush or press them to release juice. Add enough alcohol to create 18-20% alcohol juice.

1 liter of juice and 250 ml 95% alcohol will produce 19% alcohol juice. 1 liter of juice and 325 ml of 75% alcohol will create 19% alcohol juice.

This becomes your raw material for the future. Sour cherry vodka should contain about 40-50% of this juice in order to preserve the sour cherry flavor in the final product. .

Making sour cherries vodka by infusion method

Crush sour cherries, save 20% pits and place all in a jar.
Sour cherries, 250 g
75% alcohol, 500 ml

Macerate 3-4 weeks. Strain. Sour cherries produce clear juice so you may not need to filter it. Add sugar syrup, flavorings and alcohol and water.

In most cases about 25% pits are saved and added to the infusion. The pits are added whole. This imparts a slight flavor of almond which is favored by most people. Vanilla is often added.

How much sugar you add is up to you, this is your drink. Sour cherries need some sugar and 10% (100 g/l) is the safe path to take. Generally, the more sugar you add the weaker your vodka becomes. It also depends whether you use 19% alcohol juice, 40% infusion or both of them (see calculating recipes).

Plum Vodkas

Plum juice is difficult to clarify, but the infusion made from dried plums (prunes) is clear. Generally, dry fruit and berries make much clearer infusions. It must be mentioned that the highest quality plum vodkas are produced from navy blue "damson plums." However, any type of plum, even the tropical "loquat" that goes by the nickname "Chinese plum" in Florida, will produce an outstanding spirit. The plum infusion that will be used for making vodka should be supplied at 25%, this means 250 g for 1 liter of product. Infusions of 40% alcohol fruit juices 20% or even fresh juices from other plum varieties may be added. Juice from blue berries is often added for coloring.

Citrus Vodkas

When we eat our oranges or lemons, we usually peel away the thick layer of skin and remove the bitter white part, also known as pith. It is the white flesh lying under the rind, between the rind and the pulp. We do not want the pith because it is bitter. Any white membrane that covers the fruit should be discarded as well. In addition to their bitterness, the pith and membranes contain plenty of pectin (commercial pectin is produced from citrus skins). Pectin is used for making gels that we use to make jams, jellies and marmalades. Pectin is also responsible for making citrus fruit cloudy so its amount should be limited to a minimum. Discard as much pith as practically possible but save the skin for skin infusion.

Photo 4.4 Citrus pith in lemon (left), orange (right) and mandarin orange (bottom).

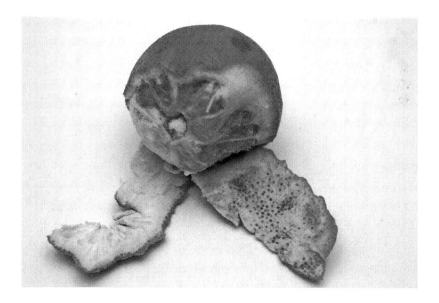

Photo 4.5 The pith was removed from the right peel and only the skin remains.

Most of the lemon or orange flavor is locked inside the skin. Juices from tropical fruits such as lemon, orange, banana and others are usually cloudy, so even a well filtered infusion may not be perfectly clear. The hardest to filter is lemon juice and even factory made lemon vodkas tend to be cloudy.

When lemons or oranges are added whole they should be separated into little wedges, and all white membranes, seeds and skins should be removed. There is a variety of tools that efficiently extract juice from lemons or oranges. There are manual juicers, lever operated squeezers and electrical models, too. Mix juice with alcohol and let it macerate. Then strain the infusion and filter.

A little lemon skin extract/infusion is usually added to orange vodkas. By the same token lemon vodka will benefit from a little orange flavor.

The easiest method to produce quality citrus vodka is to:

- Mix a natural essential oil with alcohol *OR*:
- Mix orange or lemon skin infusion with alcohol.

Using a natural essential orange oil or homemade extract infusion from lemon or orange skins will produce a perfectly clear vodka. Clear vodkas generally contain more fruit infusion and are sweeter. Their color is more intense.

Photo 4.6 Peeling off lemon skin for making skin infusion.

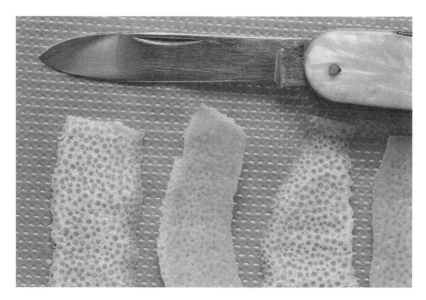

Photo 4.7 The pith can be further reduced with a knife.

Citrus juice may be preserved for future use:

150 ml fresh lemon/orange juice (about 3 fruit).

75% alcohol, 50 ml.

Macerate for 10 days, then filter. The alcohol strength of the juice is 18% which makes it safe to store.

Such juice infusions can be bottled or immediately used for making vodka.

Orange Vodkas

Oranges are not fully matured when distributed to stores. They contain a lot of flesh in their rind which decreases in time as the orange dries out. The best oranges will be fully ripened fruits, still hanging from a tree. These oranges contain very little pith. The clearest vodka is made from orange skin infusion. Adding a 10% lemon skin infusion in relation to orange skin infusion rounds out the flavor nicely. For 250 ml of orange skin infusion add 25 ml (about 2 tablespoons) of lemon skin infusion.

The basic process:

1. Make orange skin infusion.

Orange Skins	Fresh - 100 g	Dry - 100 g
Alcohol	70%, 500 ml	50%, 500 ml
Maceration Time	3 - 4 days	7 days
Remarks	Remove white under skin flesh. Strain and filter.	Strain and filter.

About 250 ml of orange skin infusion is added for making orange vodka.

2. Add sugar, spices and flavorings.

3. Add water to arrive at 40% strength.

4. Bottle and age at least 2 days.

Depending on the amount of sugar orange vodkas can be

- Dry – up to 50 g of sugar per 1 liter.
- Semi-sweet – 51-120 g/l.
- Sweet – 121-300 g/l.

Anything sweeter will be classified as a liqueur. Other ingredients which are commonly added are: lemon skin, cloves, vanilla.

Lemon Vodkas

The manufacturing of lemon vodka follows the same procedure for making orange vodka. The easiest method is just to add a few lemon skins into plain vodka and wait a few days for the flavor to set in. Use only fully matured yellow lemons. If you make lemon vodka from skins only, it will have a nice aroma and will be crystal clear. However, if you use lemon skin extract alone you will get plenty of aroma, but you will notice that the drink will benefit from more acidity. If you add lemon juice you will lose some clarity so the best approach is to add some citric acid (0.1%, 1 g/l). Taste and add more if needed. Citric acid is made from lemons so it is a natural combination. If fresh lemon juice or lemon infusion is added, adding citric acid should be avoided as the drink may become overly sour. Adding 10% *orange* skin infusion in relation to lemon skin infusion improves the flavor nicely. For 250 ml of lemon skin infusion add 25 ml (about 2 tablespoons) of *orange* skin infusion. Adding sugar is up to you but most people like between 5-10% (50-100 g/l).

Lemon skins infusion:

Lemon Skins	Fresh - 100 g	Dry - 100 g
Alcohol	70%, 500 ml	50%, 500 ml
Maceration Time	3 - 4 days	7 days
Remarks	Remove white under skin flesh. Strain and filter.	Strain and filter.

About 250 ml of lemon skin infusion is added for making lemon vodka.

Often added ingredients are ginger, orange skin, vanilla.

Grapefruit Vodkas

Grapefruits, white or pink, make wonderful vodkas and they do not need other ingredients. What is most surprising is how clear the filtered infusion comes out.

Photo 4.8 Filtered infusions, going left to right: white grapefruit, pink grapefruit, orange, lemon.

Because grapefruit infusions are crystal clear, they can be added to many sweet infusions or honey to offset some of the sweetness. Kiwi can be used for the same purpose, although grapefruit is more sour.

Locally Grown Fruit

Economics dictate that you should utilize any free fruit that you come across. There is an abundance of citrus trees in tropical states, for example in Florida. There are trees left and right with fruit that nobody cares to pick up. Use lemons, oranges, and grapefruits for making vodkas. Mandarin oranges make very good orange liqueur. Kumquats, which look like golf ball size oranges have a flavor that lies somewhere between lemon and orange and make wonderful vodkas and infusions. Save all those skins and make infusions or dry them out for later use.

Honey Vodkas

Honey vodkas should not be confused with honey wines (mead). Honey wine is fermented and contains little alcohol (12-16%), but honey vodkas are not fermented and are strong (40-50%). Aromatic infusions such as ginger, cloves, cinnamon, and nutmeg are often added as well as citric acid that offsets some of the honey's sweetness. The color of honey vodka is largely influenced by honey's color and caramel may be added to darken it. In Poland honey vodka is known as "krupnik."

Top quality honey vodka does not contain sugar at all, just honey, aromatic spices and alcohol. The more economic type will have a part of honey substituted with sugar, usually 50%. Good honey vodka should contain between 140-200 ml (200-280 g) of honey per 1 liter of product. One liter of honey weighs about 1.4 kg.

Numerous honey vodkas include a fruit infusion or alcohol enriched juice, for example raspberry, sour cherry or cherry. Adding a kiwi infusion creates excellent results.

Candy Vodkas

Candy vodkas have been around for a while and may be considered a quick way to produce fruit vodkas. Nevertheless, this method is a practical solution for those who are not particularly fond of drinking plain vodka. They are popular among the younger crowd and students who have more free time on their hands.

Any hard candy can be mixed with vodka, however, clear candies produce the clearest color. The variety of colors is due to the commercially produced food colorings which have been approved by the Food and Drugs Administration. Skittles® candies have been used in vodkas all over the world, Jolly Rancher® candies are clear and carry wonderful and distinct fruit aroma. Start with adding 10% of candy in relation to the total volume (1 liter) of 40% (80 proof) vodka. Such vodka will have the degree of sweetness that would appeal to most people. To make it sweeter, add more candy.

A good idea is to carry a selection of basic essential oil flavors. One drop of lemon, orange or peppermint oil will add more flavor to 500 ml of vodka. A dissolved candy infusion must be filtered in order to remove all impurities which were added during the candy manufacturing process. This will result in a clear color as well. Candies can be used to make liqueurs and crèmes as well, however, stay away from stuffed candies as this can produce unexpected results. Use chocolate or coffee candies instead.

Photo 4.9 Skittles® candy vodka.

Think Differently

A top quality alcoholic beverage must meet the following requirements:

- It has to taste good.
- It must have a nice and clear color.
- It should be labeled and packaged in an attractive container.
- The quality should remain constant regardless of when it was made.

First of all try to forget this nonsense of using cups, spoons, whole eggs and fruits. Spoons are different in every part of the world, cups, pints and quarts are hard to calculate, different size eggs have different weights, a small orange weighs less than a big one. You may be lucky one day, but your luck will run out the second time and the quality of your spirit will suffer.

You should not rely on luck when mixing drinks. You should rely on precise measurements. One spoon of Kosher salt weighs differently than one spoon of common table salt so depending on spoons as a unit of measure makes no sense at all. But 6 grams of salt remains always 6 grams of salt no matter whether it is measured with teaspoons or tablespoons.

To sum it up:

- Weigh your ingredients.
- Measure your liquids in a measured cylinder.
- Think metric.

The world is metric so become familiar with it. We could write all recipes in an archaic method using measurements like spoons, cups, ounces, quarts, etc. But this will be cheating you as you will never understand the subject and you will never be able to calculate your own recipes. As you keep on reading, you will see that calculating your own recipes is very simple. Your new world where you should move around now is called one liter. It consists of 1,000 small parts called milliliters. One milliliter of water weighs exactly 1 gram, so 1 liter must weigh 1,000 grams. You can already see how simple it becomes.

You decide how to distribute this volume of space, how many milliliters alcohol will occupy and how many milliliters are dedicated to sugar. If you introduce a fresh juice to the drink, it is up to you to decide how much space will be given to it. You have a total of 1,000 milliliters to spare and you decide how to use the space. Think of a building a house whose interior space cannot exceed 1,000 square feet. You have to decide how to fill it with rooms, bathrooms, size of the kitchen, closets and anything else. All those components cannot exceed 1,000 square feet.

This is how you create your drinks, you have 1,000 milliliters of space and you decide what and how much goes inside. And when your total is a few milliliters short, you add plain water to make it exactly 1,000 milliliters (1 liter).

It is almost impossible not to create a good recipe using good fruit and alcohol. Many things can go wrong when one makes wine, for example frequent exposure to air can promote vinegar yeasts to develop and the product will be sour. Making infusions is very reliable as fermentation does not take place and alcohol inhibits bacteria growth. The product will simply not go bad, have you ever heard of a spoiled vodka or whisky? In short, we do not have safety concerns which we must face like the meat industry.

Basically a recipe is a combination of alcohol and fruit, herbs, sugar or other ingredients. In the case of plain vodkas it is just alcohol and water. The manipulation of sugar is simple, you add enough until you are satisfied. Or use percentages, having 150 g of sugar in 1 liter of vodka means we have 15% sugar. Adding 400 g means that we have 40% of sugar. One liter of sugar weighs 1056 grams.

It is like a pizza pie, it has a fixed boundary but you can do whatever you like inside. The boundary in alcohol making is 1 liter. The factory will have a bigger pie, for example 100 liters, but as long as it is in magnitudes of 10 (1, 10, 100) it is easy to calculate.

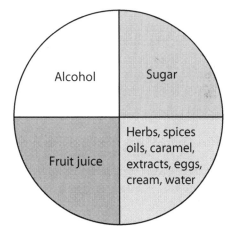

Fig. 4.3 All ingredients link together.

Make note that changing any single ingredient affects the others. For example, if we decrease the amount of juice, we have to add something else, even water; otherwise the bottle will only be partially filled. If we increase the amount of juice, amount of sugar or add a new component, we have to readjust the other components otherwise we will decrease the alcoholic strength of the drink and the flavor of the spirit. Besides we will end up with more drink than can fit into a 1 liter bottle.

Use of Essential Oils

General guidelines:

Essential oils should be considered just another tool for making spirits. Essential oils are liquids extracted from highly fragrant plants and flowers. They have been around for thousands of years for a variety of uses including medicinal and cooking.

The ones that are of interest to us for making alcohol type beverages are produced by:

- Cold pressing. This method is used to extract oils from lemon and orange skins. The oils are yellow.

- Steam distillation. Water is boiled to create steam, which then travels through a bunch of herbs. The steam breaks the structure of herbs, extracts oil, and then flows into the condenser. There, it becomes a liquid solution of water and oil and goes into a separator. The oil being lighter than water is physically separated and the water is discarded. The oils are clear.

Essential oils work well for making dry vodkas. Adding 1 ml of oil to one liter of 40% alcohol delivers the necessary flavor and does not create cloudiness. Adding more oil can be problematic and will start to impart cloudiness. The cloudiness will generally clear in time but will reappear when the bottle is shaken.

Using oils is a perfect solution for commercial producers who have huge supplies of alcohol. All they need to do is to dilute alcohol to 40%, add 1 ml of essential oil and flavored vodka is produced. As the steam essential oils are clear approved food coloring is added. Orange oil carries a yellow color as it has been made by cold pressing and not by steam distillation, however, it is added in a such a diminutive quantity that the resulting vodka remains clear. A yellow color can be obtained by adding saffron or an approved food coloring. Peppermint oil will impart peppermint but the vodka will be clear. As people associate mint with a green color, green food grade coloring is added.

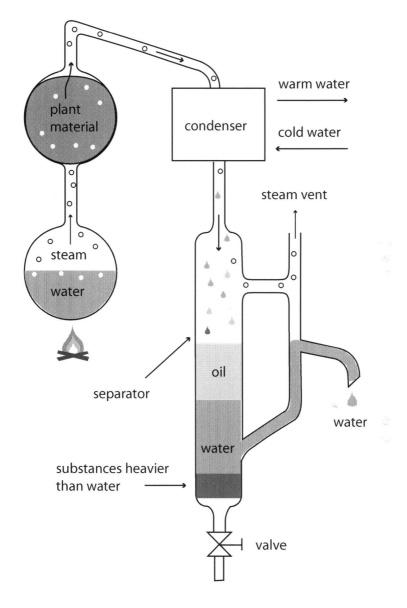

Fig. 4.4 Producing essential oils by steam distillation.

Infusions produce much better vodkas than using oils alone. Infusion is the wrench and essential oil is just a socket. Oils supply plenty of aroma, but infusions carry more of the fruit's natural flavor. Caraway vodka made by the infusion process carries its own natural color and tastes better than the clear caraway vodka that was produced with caraway oil alone. In addition, each fruit or herb stamps the infusion with its natural flavor, for example papaya infusion retains papaya's color and the same is true with cherry, strawberry and other infusions. Surprisingly, white and pink grapefruits turn out crystal clear.

Nevertheless, a small collection of essential oils becomes a powerful weapon in your arsenal. Every popular herb and spice can be obtained in the form of essential oil so they become of great value for experimenting with bitter vodkas or herbal liqueurs. They can be added at any time to boost the flavor of the infusion. Let's say you have a peppermint infusion. It has an acceptable color but you feel that it lacks some mint flavor. All you need to do is add a drop or two of peppermint oil and the aroma will be much stronger. Generally, you do not need more than 1/2 ml of essential oil for 1 liter of infusion to magnify the flavor.

Chapter 5

Liqueurs and Crèmes

Liqueurs

Until the discovery of distillation the art of making liqueurs was not known. Wine and beer were common but did not contain sufficient amounts of alcohol to fully extract flavors from fruits, herbs and spices. When the first alembic had appeared we started to produce strong alcohols, but that knowledge was reserved for the clergy. In those times monasteries were the centers of human science and monks were always looking for some magical drinks and powders. Not surprisingly, they were the first ones to soak herbs and spices in alcohols creating what is known today as infusions. Eventually, some monks went a step further and distilled such an infusion. To everyone's surprise it turned out to be clear having a new aroma and flavor. This led to more experiments and many new drinks were created. The best example is Dom Bénédictine or Chartreuse liqueurs, the last one consisting of over 120 different herbs and spices. Those early liqueurs were herbal medicines; they were made as early as the 13th century and were usually prepared by monks. Nowadays, liqueurs are very popular and don't necessarily require distilling equipment to produce them.

A liqueur is an alcoholic beverage made from distilled alcohol that has been flavored with fruit, cream, herbs, spices, flowers or nuts and bottled with added sugar. Liqueurs are usually sweet drinks that contain over 330 g/l sugar. This definition is not set in stone and what some may call sweet vodka, others may think of as a liqueur. Liqueurs do exhibit certain characteristics that differentiate them from other drinks. First, they are bottled in original containers; they carry fancy labels and closures. Secondly, they incorporate dessert types of ingredients such as chocolate, cacao, coffee, cream and aromatic essential oils. One can make orange vodka by adding 10% of sugar or one can make orange liqueur by adding 30% sugar.

Original liqueurs were quite strong, for example Dom Bénédictine had an alcohol content of 43%, however, consumer preferences are changing and as of late it is made at 40%. The sweeter the liqueur is, the lower alcohol content it carries, as there is less available space to add alcohol, especially if one has access to 75% alcohol only.

The hardest liqueurs to make are herb liqueurs which require sophisticated combinations of herbs, spices, dry flowers and time. For example, **Dom Bénédictine** liqueur was invented by Alexandre Le Grand, a wine merchant and industrialist in 1863 after he stumbled in the library of the abbey of Fécamp on an old herbal recipe collected by the monks of the abbey. The recipe looked reliable yet somewhat unusual. Via the aid of a pharmacist he refined the recipe and created the liqueur that would make him famous. The recipe incorporates over 20 spices and is a closely guarded trade secret, ostensibly known to only three people at any given time.

Another classic, **Chartreuse**, is a French liqueur made by the Carthusian Monks since the 1740's. It is composed of distilled alcohol aged with 130 herbal extracts. The liqueur is named after the Monks' Grande Chartreuse monastery, located in the Chartreuse Mountains in the region of Grenoble in France.

There are two types of Chartreuse:

Green Chartreuse (55%), is a naturally green liqueur flavored with extracts from 132 plants with its coloring coming from chlorophyll.

Yellow Chartreuse (40%), which has a milder and sweeter flavor and aroma.

Chartreuse liqueur is credited with the naming of Chartreuse color, halfway between yellow and green, it was named because of its resemblance to the green color of one of the French liqueurs called green chartreuse, introduced in 1764. The term chartreuse was first used to refer to "apple-green" in 1884. This was codified to refer to a brighter green color when the X11 colors were formulated in 1987; by the early 1990's, they became known as the X11 web colors. The web color chartreuse is the color precisely halfway between green and yellow, so it is 50% green and 50% yellow.

To summarize, some liqueurs have a long history and it will be impossible to duplicate the recipe. Making liqueurs provides unlimited possibilities for a creative person who is keen on inventing new beverages.

Many liqueurs such as Cointreau and Royal Mint Chocolate are clear liquids. We could obtain a clear liqueur even from coffee or cacao beans but that will require distillation, a process which is not permitted in home production.

Liqueurs need time to mellow. They often contain many ingredients and some of them may stand out when a liqueur has just been made. Given time, all ingredients blend in together creating the unified harmony of flavors. For example, Chartreuse and Benedictine mature for at least 3 years in oak casks.

Liqueurs require top quality ingredients. The recipes are more complicated and they cost more to produce. Creating a good liqueur requires some experience and the process is more involved than making a fruit infusion.

Liqueurs may be classified into a few groups:

- Herbal liqueurs - Dom Bénédictine, Chatreuse, Goldwasser. These are strong spirits around 40% alcohol, 400 g/l sugar. Infusions are made with 50-55% alcohol. It is difficult to generalize the amount of dry roots, herbs and spices for an herb liqueur. People in different countries exhibit different likings, for example in Austria or Germany there is a preference for very aromatic and bitter liqueurs which call for 100-300 g of herbs to 10 l of product. In other countries little herbs are added, about 10-50 g/10 l which results in a more subtle flavor.

- Bitter liqueurs - Stondsdorfer, Boonekamp, 32-40%. These are very bitter liqueurs and it is improbable that a person will take them in a large quantity. A drink or two is taken before a meal as it is considered an herbal remedy, an aperitif that stimulates the appetite and helps digest the food.

Fruit liqueurs - Cherry Liqueur, Cherry-Brandy, Cassis, Maraschino, Peter Heering Cherry Liqueur. Fruit liqueurs contain less alcohol, 25-35%.

- Liqueurs made from citrus fruit fit into this group, for example Cointreau.

- Liqueurs with a distinctive, original flavor - Amaretto almond liqueur, Kahlua and Tia Maria coffee liqueurs. Those liqueurs contain about 25-32% alcohol.

Herbal Liqueurs

These are sweet and strong liqueurs averaging around 400 g sugar/l and 40% alcohol. *Bitter herbal vodkas may not appeal to most of us, however, the large amount of sugar that is added to liqueurs transforms the spirit into something completely different and delicious.*

1. Take herbs/spices and macerate for 2 weeks with 50% alcohol. In most cases you will be using dry herbs which are known to retain a lot of alcohol. It is a good habit to create aromatic and herb infusions in the ratio of 1 part dry herbs to 10 parts of alcohol. For 10 g dry herbs take 100 ml of alcohol. After straining you are not going to obtain 100 ml of infusion as the herbs are holding quite a lot of alcohol. You can compensate for that by:

Adding 50% more alcohol, eg. around 150 ml 50% alcohol and 10 g of dry herbs OR

- Making two infusions: the first one with 100 ml alcohol, 10 g dry herbs. Macerate 2 weeks, strain the liquid.

- The second infusion: add 50 ml alcohol to the same herbs, macerate for 2 weeks, strain the liquid.

- Combine both infusions together.

You should obtain about 100 ml infusion and each 10 ml corresponds to 1 gram of dry herbs.

2. Such an infusion becomes your base material for making a liqueur. You may create your own favorite combinations. Usually you will need 30-40 ml (3-4%) of such an infusion for making 1 liter of liqueur. The rest will be sugar syrup 73%, 400 ml (40%), and 525 ml (52.5%) 75%

alcohol, other ingredients and possibly some water to bring the liqueur to the 1 liter mark. The strength of such liqueur is 40% alcohol.

3. Bottle and age. The older it is, the better it becomes.

4. Always label every bottle and remember to date it. Keep detailed records.

Fruit liqueurs and citrus fruit liqueurs follow the same rules which were presented in making fruit vodkas in Chapter 4. The main difference is liqueurs contain around 40% sugar (400 g/l).

Liqueurs With a Distinctive Original Flavor

Most of those liqueurs, such as caraway, mint and anise are popular in less sweet vodka versions. Others like cacao or coffee liqueurs are made using a typical infusion/vodka making process:

1. Making cacao or coffee infusion. Take 100 g ground cacao or coffee beans and macerate for 2 weeks in 1000 ml of 50% alcohol. Filter and bottle.

2. Use as a base material for making a liqueur. Follow recipes.

Crèmes

The consistency of crèmes and sweet liqueurs are thicker. This is obtained by introducing:

* More sugar - sugar is a thickening agent.
* Eggs - an egg is an emulsifying and thickening agent. On occasion heavy cream is added.

Type	Alcohol Strength %	Sugar g/l	Material
Sweet	20 - 28	500 - 550	Crème de Cassis (black currants), Crème de banana (banana), Crème de Cacao (cacao), Crème de Mocca
Emulsion	16 - 25	400 - 450	Advocaat (egg yolk)

Dutch Advocaat has been known all over the world. This crème owes its popularity to:

- The ease of preparation.
- Wonderful taste.

Polish Eiercognac

The Polish equivalent called ajerkoniak (Eier - egg in German, Cognac - French for brandy) is based on vodka instead of brandy, despite what the name may suggest.

This is a simple and more economical version of Advocaat. Originally, it was made in a baked clay bowl known as "makutra" that was used for grounding poppy seeds or sugar with egg yolks to make pastries and cakes. It may be considered a large "mortar and pestle" set, where the mortar is the clay bowl and the pestle is a heavy wooden club with a ball at the end. The set works surprisingly well and has been used for centuries for grinding materials into paste.

Photo 5.1 Makutra mixing bowl.

Photo 5.2 Separating egg yolks from whites.

Photo 5.3 Adding yolks to sugar.

Photo 5.4 Egg yolks and sugar ready to mix.

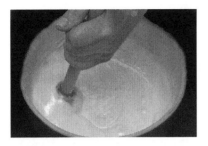

Photo 5.5 Grinding egg yolks with sugar. Superfine sugar makes the operation easier.

Photo 5.6 When eggs and sugar become paste, the alcohol can be slowly added.

Your tongue should not feel any particles of sugar, the cream must be completely smooth. Then alcohol is slowly added and the mixture is continuously stirred. Adding alcohol rapidly may break down the emulsion.

Let us make something absolutely clear, an electric mixer will not make a better egg crème than a manual "makutra." The saving is only in time and in ease of operation. Having used both equipment on many occasions, I am inclined to say that "makutra" makes much smoother crème.

Keep in mind that vanilla pods are impossible to grind, they tend to remain little rubbery pieces. Use vanilla extract instead.

Take your time with an electric mixer. Do not assume that the mixture is smooth, operate the mixer for at least 5 minutes. You can use sugar syrup which will

Photo 5.7 Electric mixer.

produce a thinner mixture. Add another egg yolk to compensate. Occasionally a layer of white foam will appear on top of a freshly made crème. These are the tiny air bubbles that were formed during mixing but will disappear the next day.

Photo 5.8 From left: Advocaat, Polish Eiercognac, Egg Cream.

Advocaat includes a small amount of rum and cognac, but this is enough to give it a distinct flavor. Egg crèmes made with heavy cream are lighter, thinner and weaker.

Egg emulsion crèmes are often made with cacao or coffee infusions. About 400 ml cacao/coffee infusion, 6-8 eggs (100 g), 400 ml sugar syrup 73% (400 g sugar), and 100 ml of 75% alcohol.

Contests

There are many conventions and trade fairs and this contest is often one of the main attractions. People submit their creations, whether they be infusions, vodkas or liqueurs in hopes of winning prizes and recognition. At the 7th Annual Sausage Makers Convention that takes place in August in Poland there were 40 entries. The bottles were wrapped with aluminum foil and a panel of six judges was selected. The judges are chosen among people who are known for their life-long commitment to heavy drinking and their thorough knowledge of the subject. The spirits were evaluated by color, clarity, flavor and aroma. After two rounds of drinking the judges selected three finalists. Some of the spirits were so good that it was hard to choose the winner. This only reinforces the point that you don't need factory equipment to create outstanding spirits, and the truth is that factories cannot create drinks to match the quality of those created by a dedicated homeowner.

Photo 5.9 Bottles are wrapped with aluminum foil for blind testing.

Photo 5.10 The judges at work.

Chapter 6

Calculating Recipes

Alcoholic drinks are liquids and are measured by volume. The main unit of measurement is one liter which consists of one thousand milliliters. Imagine that you have a thousand little cubes and they occupy a volume of one liter. If your drink contains 50% alcohol by volume it means that half of the space is filled with alcohol and the rest with something else, which may be juice, sugar or water. So when you see 1 liter bottle of 40% (80-proof) vodka that means that 400 ml (40%) is pure alcohol and 600 ml (60%) is something else. By the same token, if you see ½ liter (500 ml) bottle of 40% vodka that means that there is 200 ml (40%) of pure alcohol and 300 ml (60%) of something else. Let's check:

40% x 500/100% = 200 ml pure alcohol which we can write as 200 ml 100%

60% x 500/100% = 300 ml

This brings us to the frequent discussion about what is the best drink to take and not get drunk; vodka, wine or beer? Let us compare beer and vodka.

Beer – 500 ml, 6% alcohol

6 x 500/100 = 30 ml of pure 100% alcohol in each 500 ml bottle of beer.

Vodka – 30 ml vodka glass, 40% alcohol

40 x 30/100 = 12 ml of pure 100% alcohol in each 30 ml glass of vodka.

Well, it is surprising to find out that someone would have to drink 25 shots of vodka to match 10 beers.

Ten beers contain: 10 x 30 ml of 100% alcohol = 300 ml 100% alcohol total.

300ml/12ml (100% alcohol in vodka glass) = 25 glasses of vodka

Let's see how big of a vodka glass is needed to match 500 ml 6% beer.

From Chapter 1, The Magic Equation

$C1V1 = C2V2$

40% x V1 = 6% x 500

V1 = 6x500/40 = 75 ml

500 ml bottle of 6% beer = 75 ml glass of 40% vodka.

The conclusion is that it does not really matter much what you drink, but rather how much.

Creating Recipes

Example 1

Peach Vodka, 40%, 1 liter

Ingredients:

Peach infusion, 300 ml, 50%

White wine, 200 ml, 15%

Sugar, 100 g

Caramel, 5 g

Alcohol 75% - ? This will be added later to bring the strength of vodka to 40%. (In Europe we will choose 95% alcohol but in the USA we can get only 75%).

Water - ? A small amount is usually added at the end to round up the volume of vodka to 1 liter.

Analysis: Our intention is to produce a 40% vodka so we need 400 ml (40%) of pure 100% alcohol. Let's see how much alcohol we already have, then we will make up the difference with 75% alcohol.

Peach infusion – 50x300/100 = 15000/100 = 150 ml 100%

White wine – 15x200/100 = 3000/100 = 30 ml 100%

So far, we have 150 ml of 100% alcohol in peach infusion + 30 ml of 100% alcohol in white wine and this gives us the total of 150 + 30 = 180 ml of 100% alcohol. In other words if we now mix 300 ml of peach infusion, 200 ml of white wine and 500 ml of water we would obtain 1 liter of 18% spirit. However, we are aiming to produce 1 liter of 40% peach vodka which requires 400 ml of 100% alcohol. To meet this goal we have to add more alcohol.

We have 150 ml (peach infusion) + 30 ml (white wine) of alcohol = 180 ml 100%. We need the total of 400 ml 100% so we have to add: 400 – 180 = 220 ml of 100% alcohol. You add the strongest alcohol that there is available, in our case 75%. It is obviously weaker (contains water) than pure 100% alcohol so the amount will be larger than 220 ml 100%.

C1xV1=C2xV2

75 x V1 = 100 x 220

V1 = 100x220/75 = 293 ml

We need to add 293 ml of 75% alcohol.

Let's add all we have:

Peach infusion, 300 ml, 50%

White wine, 200 ml, 15%

Sugar, 100 g (we will use 100 ml 73% sugar syrup)

Caramel, 5 g (we will use 5 ml caramel syrup)

Alcohol 75%, 293 ml

300 + 200 + 100 +5 + 293 =

Total: 898 ml.

Water - ?

We are making 1 liter (1000 ml) of vodka so we need add water.

$1000 - 898 = 102$ ml.

We need 102 ml of water.

Note: if we don't add water we will end up with 898 ml of 44% vodka and this is not what we planned.

The best method is to have a graduated cylinder or marked container with a 1 liter mark. Then we add all our components and we top it off with water to the 1 liter mark. To round up the volume to 1 liter, we may use fruit juice instead of water.

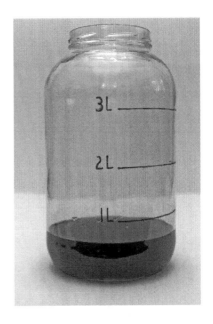

Photo 6.1 Graduated jar for mixing components.

We will follow with more examples, but the basic steps are:

1. Choose the strength of your drink.

2. Decide how sweet you want it to be.

3. Calculate how much 100% alcohol you already have.

4. Calculate how much more 100% alcohol you need to add. Then find the equivalent amount of 75% alcohol.

5. Add all components together.

6. Top it off with water or juice to the 1 liter mark.

Perform your calculations for 1 liter, it is easier that way. Then if you need more spirit, just multiply everything by a factor of 2, 3, 5 or 10. It is your recipe and you are in charge. You can change any of the ingredients at will. All you have to remember is that your drink consists of 1000 little parts called milliliters and everything else will fall in place.

Example 2

Honey Vodka - Krupnik, 50%, 1 liter.

Raspberry infusion, 50 ml, 40%

Honey, 300 ml

Lemon juice, 5 ml (1 tsp.)

Alcohol 75%

Water

Analysis:

1. Desired strength 50%, this means we need 500 ml of 100% alcohol.

2. The amount of sugar, around 300 g.

3. Alcohol we have, raspberry infusion, 40 ml, 40%.

40x50/100 = 20 ml.

Alcohol in raspberry infusion corresponds to 20 ml of 100% alcohol.

4. We need to add more 100% alcohol.

500 ml – 20 ml = 480 ml.

We need to add 480 ml of 100% alcohol.

Using 75% alcohol:

C1xV1 = C2 x V2

100 x 480 = 75 x V2

V2 = 100 x 480/75 = 640 ml

We need to add 640 ml of 75% alcohol.

5. Adding all up:

40 ml Raspberry + 300 ml honey + 5 ml lemon juice + 640 ml 75% alcohol = 985 ml

5. Adding 15 ml water will bring the volume to 1 liter.

Note: honey is heavier than water. 1 liter of water weighs 1 kg. I liter

of honey weighs 1.425 kg.

Example 3

Honey - Cherry Liqueur, 30%, 1 liter

Honey, 200 ml (280 g)

Cherry infusion, 300 ml, 40%

Citric acid, 1 g OR 1 teaspoon of lemon juice (5 ml)

Sugar syrup (73%), 200 ml (200 g)

Alcohol 75%

Water

Analysis:

1. Desired strength 30%, this means we need 300 ml of 100% alcohol.

2. The amount of sugar (honey included), around 400 g.

3. Alcohol we have, cherry infusion, 300 ml, 40%.

40x300/100 = 120 ml

Alcohol in cherry infusion corresponds to 120 ml of 100% alcohol.

4. We need to add more 100% alcohol.

300 ml – 120 ml = 180 ml.

We need to add 180 ml of 100% alcohol.

Using 75% alcohol:

C1 x V1 = C2 x V2

100 x 180 = 75 x V2

V2 = 100 x 180/75 = 240 ml

We need to add 240 ml of 75% alcohol.

5. Adding all up:

200 ml honey + 300 ml Cherry + 5 ml lemon juice + 200 ml sugar syrup + 240 ml 75% alcohol = 945 ml

5. Adding 55 ml water will bring the volume to 1 liter.

Example 4

Ratafia, 30%, 1 liter

Raspberry infusion, 100 ml, 40%

Sour cherry infusion, 200 ml, 40%

Strawberry infusion, 300 ml, 40%

Sugar syrup (73%), 200 ml (200 g)

Vanilla infusion 2 ml (0.2%)

Alcohol 75%

Water

1. Desired strength 30%, this means we need 300 ml of 100% alcohol.

2. The amount of sugar, 200 g.

3. Alcohol we have, raspberry infusion, 100 ml, 40%.

40x100/100 = 40 ml

Alcohol in raspberry infusion corresponds to 40 ml of 100% alcohol.

Sour cherry infusion, 40x200/100 = 80 ml

Alcohol in sour cherry infusion corresponds to 80 ml of 100% alcohol.

Strawberry infusion, 40x300/100 = 120 ml

Alcohol in strawberry infusion corresponds to 120 ml of 100% alcohol.

Total 100% alcohol we have, 40 + 80 + 120 = 240 ml

4. We need to add more 100% alcohol.

300 ml – 240 ml = 60 ml.

We need to add 60 ml of 100% alcohol.

Using 75% alcohol:

C1xV1 = C2 x V2

100 x 60 = 75 x V2

V2 = 100 x 60/75 = 80 ml

We need to add 80 ml of 75% alcohol.

5. Adding all up:

100 ml raspberry + 200 ml sour cherry + 300 ml strawberry + 200 ml sugar syrup + 80 ml 75% alcohol + 2 ml vanilla = 882 ml

5. 1000 ml – 882 ml = 118 ml. Adding 118 ml water will bring the volume to 1 liter.

Composing recipes in this way is crucial if making large quantities of spirit, like 10 liters and for consistent results. Sprinkling sugar over fruit and pouring vodka over it is fine for making a quart of spirit but not a few gallons. Even if you decide to use your own methods, it is nice to know that you can write up a professional recipe at any time.

Liqueurs and Crèmes

Fruit liqueurs should have a distinct accented flavor so adding water must be restricted to a minimum. The dominant flavor may come from infusion or alcohol fruit juice and should account for about 30% of the total.

Example 5

Cherry Liqueur, 30%, 1 liter

Cherry infusion, 350 ml, 40%

Sugar syrup (73%), 400 ml

Vanilla infusion, 2 ml

75% alcohol

Water

Analysis: cherry infusion contains:

$40 \times 350/100 = 140$ ml 100% alcohol

The intended strength of 1 liter cherry liqueur is 30%. This requires

300 ml of 100% alcohol.

$300 - 140$ ml $= 160$

We have to add 160 ml of 100% alcohol to make our liqueur 30%. We have to use 75% as this type is available to us in the USA.

$C1V1 = C2V2$

$100 \times 160 = 75 \times V2$

$V2 = 100 \times 160/75 = 213$ ml 75% alcohol.

We need to add 213 ml of 75% alcohol.

Adding it all up:

350 ml cherry infusion + 400 ml sugar syrup + 2 ml vanilla + 213 ml 75% alcohol = 965 ml.

We need to add 35 ml of water (1000 – 965 = 35).

Note: instead of 35 ml of water a juice may be added, for example raspberry.

On occasion you may decide to increase the amount of a particular ingredient, for example instead of adding 35 ml water, you will add 85 ml of juice. This pushes you over the 1 liter mark by 50 ml. You must compensate by readjusting the amounts of other ingredients, for example decreasing the amount of sugar syrup by 50 ml. Lowering the amount of sugar syrup to 350 ml allows you to add 85 ml of juice and still keep the volume at 1 liter. Take under consideration that adding or removing an ingredient that contains alcohol may affect the strength of the spirit.

Egg crèmes are usually weaker because sugar and egg yolks occupy a significant portion of the total volume:

Sugar – 400 ml

Egg yolks – 200 ml

Total: 400 + 200 = 600 ml.

This leaves only 400 ml (1000 – 600 = 400) of available volume for other ingredients. Even if all this 400 ml was filled with 75% alcohol the strength of the crème will be only 30%.

75 x 400/100 = 300 ml of 100% alcohol.

Which is fine as crèmes don't taste good when stronger than 30% that due to the fact that strong alcohol overpowers the flavor of eggs, coffee or chocolate.

Using 95% alcohol gives us more room to maneuver; unfortunately in the USA we are limited to 75% alcohol. This is why it is important to understand the recipe structure as we can readjust the amounts of ingredients and create liqueurs of the strength that we like.

It is much harder to calculate the precise amount of alcohol in infusions. Fruits are covered with different strength alcohols and we can only roughly estimate how much juice was obtained. The juice, of course, lowers the strength of the spirit. Filtering and weighing infusion does not help much as an unknown amount of alcohol remains in the fruit.

We can obtain good results when treating infusions as a raw material for making vodka. We can estimate the strength of the infusion by tasting it. Besides, if we macerate fruit with 70% alcohol, we should get close to a 30-40% infusion. Then we can apply our calculations to meet our target.

Making Notes

Keeping records generates an invaluable source of information for the future. Do every recipe in 1, 2 or 3 liter increments as this makes the calculations easier. Write everything down in a notebook and date it. Also make a label and stick it on the bottle with tape. Mention the ingredients, the alcohol strength, the amounts and remember to put a date on it. It is easier to read it right on the jar instead of flipping through pages in a notebook. The drinks are made and consumed, the bottles are washed and filled with new combinations and this knowledge will be wasted unless it is written down in a notebook.

About Recipes

After making a few drinks you will see that all alcohol types follow a similar procedure. You will feel how the recipe will taste once it becomes a ready to consume spirit. By tasting a new fruit infusion you will instinctively know how much sugar it needs. Then, a breakthrough will come and one day you realize that you don't need the recipe at all. You will simply know how to make different alcohol type beverages. However, in order to be assured of constant quality spirits always write down what has been done as this becomes your private reference source. This will become a simple task as long as you think in metric terms and make your beverages in 1 liter volumes.

1. Keep your infusions simple. Only then you will discover the flavor and aroma of each fruit or herb. If you make an alcohol infusion from pineapple without adding anything else, you will sense its characteristics and you will feel what other fruits, spices or herbs may go well with it. For example cinnamon goes always well with apples, oranges with cloves and so on. If you make a pure raspberry infusion, you will see that it is simply beautiful, but overly sweet and it asks for a little lemon, so is the case with honey. A little lemon juice or citric acid will balance the sweetness. When you make an infusion where everything goes into the jar together, it is like cooking a meat stew in a big pot. When you throw in everything together, you may obtain a wonderful drink today, but the trick is to have the same result every time.

2. Use a graduated jar or a mixing cylinder marked with a 1 liter level. As you place all the ingredients you will see that the volume will usually be under the 1 liter mark. This is due to alcohol contraction which was explained in Chapter 1. Simply add more water until you reach the 1 liter mark. Only then will your drink agree with your calculated recipe. If the volume is below 1 liter, the spirit will be stronger and sweeter, if it passes the mark it will be more diluted.

3. Make a habit of tasting everything. Don't just add ingredients according to the recipe, taste it. An orange that came from Guatemala, Spain, Italy, Florida or California has a different degree of sweetness and aroma. In time you will feel what will go best with it. Before you mix a new herb or spice infusion with a large amount of alcohol, run a little sample. Make only 100 ml of the beverage and see how you like it. For example, wormwood is a crucial ingredient of all herbal infusions and liqueurs. Try it on its own and you will see that it is awfully bitter. Spices like nutmeg or cardamom taste great but they can easily overpower your drink. When unsure, take only 10% infusion and make only 10% of vodka, adding of course the corresponding amount of the other ingredients. Working this way you will be able to fine tune your recipe. Just decrease everything ten times, it is that simple.

4. If you look at vodka recipes, you will see that they all start with an infusion (no sugar) and the infusion becomes the basic ingredient of the vodka. Then, all other ingredients are added and all is blended together. The recipes are simple but varied and are meant to be the foundation on which you may build your own knowledge of the subject. After reading the book you should be able to invent your own drinks on the fly, using the book as a reference once in a while only.

5. How strong and sweet your drink will be is entirely up to you. Remember only that dry drinks such as vodkas are usually strong

(40%) and they contain very little sugar and flavorings. Then, as the amount of flavorings or infusions increases, the drinks also require more sugar. For example, strawberry or raspberry infusions made without sugar do not taste so great, but once sugar is added they are delicious. Usually the sweet drinks are sweeter and darker with a more intense flavor but have a lower alcohol content.

You could manipulate recipes and make them 40% or stronger but there is a danger of overpowering the flavor characteristics of a particular fruit. In a strong drink the alcohol takes over the taste buds and we cannot feel the flavor and aroma of a particular fruit. Making your infusions at 30-40% alcohol will bring the best results. You could make them weaker still but what is the point? If you want to drink wine, buy fruit, add yeasts and make wine. Making wines is much cheaper than making vodkas, infusions or liqueurs. The latter products require the addition of alcohol which must be bought in stores. Alcohol is expensive so use it wisely.

6. Filtered infusions can be made into dry vodka, sweet vodka or liqueur. Basically only the amount of sugar differentiates vodka from liqueur. Fruit liqueurs tend to display lower alcohol strengths. Herbal liqueurs, however, taste great when they are strong. Varying the amount of sugar and alcohol of the same recipe can produce different types of liquor. You can take any fruit and make it into dry, semi-sweet, sweet vodka or liqueur. Suddenly the world of spirits that you can make has grown enormously larger. When you consider that different fruits can be mixed together and that there are hundreds of herbs and spices, the only limit is your imagination. Study good cookbooks, professional chefs choose fruits that go well together. Commercial producers invested money and effort to blend certain juices together. You can follow those combinations to make your own beverages.

7. Most recipes end with the first infusion, but by now you should know that you can follow with the second infusion. This will save a lot of infusion (and money) but makes the process longer.

- 1st infusion – fruit and alcohol. Macerate, filter and bottle.
- 2nd infusion – use leftover fruit. Add sugar and alcohol. This time you add less alcohol and at a lower strength. Macerate, filter and bottle.

You can:

- Combine both infusions together.
- Keep them as two separate drinks.

The first infusion is of better quality. You can add sugar syrup to it at any time to make it ready for consumption or you can store it for future use. The first infusion is preferred for making vodkas as it does not contain sugar. It is preserved with alcohol so there is no need to refrigerate.

8. The recipes do not mention the fact that all jars and containers should be closed tight. This is of course done to prevent the loss of alcohol through evaporation.

The processing instructions state "strain and filter." There is plenty of information on filtering in Chapter 2 and 3, and mentioning details in recipes will only crowd them.

The minimum recommended aging times are given. The longer time, the better quality of a beverage.

9. Keep detailed records for the future. Always write the weight of the fruit, the volume, the strength of the alcohol, and the date. Write this information on the jar and in the notebook.

10. Certain ingredients are used more than others. You should have a private stock of common herb and spice infusions. They should be filtered, bottled and always ready. Having that, you will be able to create a drink at a moment's notice. It is recommended to stock the following extracts/infusions: vanilla, cinnamon, nutmeg, cloves, star anise, lemon and orange skins, and ready to apply sugar syrup.

There are a few recipes that call for berries that are not known to most people. For example, edible dogwood also known as Cornelian cherry, hawthorn, blackthorn also known as sloe (*Prunus spinosa*) or rowan (mountain ash).

Those berries prefer cold climates and grow in Europe and in northern parts of the USA. They can be bought as dried berries online and a list of suppliers can be found at the end of the book. It may take some time to order them, however, the effort is well worth it as those berries produce superior vodkas.

Chapter 7

Recipe Index

#	Infusions	Page
1	Apple	167
2	Apricot, dry	168
3	Apricot, fresh	168
4	Aromatic	169
5	Bakalia	170
6	Banana	171
7	Banana-Strawberry	172
8	Black tea	173
9	Blueberries	174
10	Cherry	175
11	Chocolate	176
12	Elderberry	177
13	Ginger-Honey	178
14	Ginger-Lemon	179
15	Grapefruit	180
16	Griotte	181
17	Hawthorne	182
18	Horseradish	183
19	Kiwi	184
20	Lemon-Coffee	185
21	Linden-Rose	186
22	Loquat	187
23	Mango	188
24	Oriental	189
25	Papaya	190
26	Peach	191

59	Pepper	223
60	Peppermint	223
61	Peppermint-Herbal	224
62	Plum	225
63	Porter	226
64	Prunela	227
65	Rowan	228
66	Skittles	229
67	Sour Cherry	230
68	Sour Cherry-Ratafia	231
69	Vermouth	232
70	Walnut	233
71	Wormwood	235
Liqueurs		
72	Allasch	236
73	Amaretto	237
74	Anise	238
75	Banana-Chocolate	239
76	Benedictine	240
77	Cacao	241
78	Calamus	242
79	Chartreuse	243
80	Cherry-Chocolate	244
81	Chocolate-Mint	245
82	Coffee	246
83	Coffee-Orange	247
84	Cranberry-Ginger	248
85	English	249
86	Goldwasser	250
87	Kahlua	251
88	Kiwi-Coffee	252
89	Kumquat	253
90	Loquat	254

91	Mandarin	255
92	Orange-Cloves	256
93	Orange-Spice	257
94	Persico	258
95	Pineapple	259
96	Raspberry	260
97	Raspberry-Kiwi	261
98	Vanilla	262
Crèmes		
99	Arabica	263
100	Butterscotch	264
101	Cacao	265
102	Cassis	266
103	Chocolate	267
104	Egg	268
105	Egg with Cream	269
106	Polish Eiercognac	270
107	Vanilla	270

Infusions

Apple Infusion

Apples, 500 g

Alcohol 70%, 500 ml

Star anise (*Illicium verum*), 1 star

Cinnamon stick, 2 cm

Sugar syrup 73%, 250 ml

1. Remove the skin and seeds. Dice apples into smaller chunks.

2. Place apples, cinnamon and anise star in a jar. Add alcohol.

3. Macerate for 3 weeks. Shake jar twice a week.

4. Strain and filter. Add sugar syrup.

5. Bottle and age for one month.

Dry Apricot

Alcohol 50%, 700 ml

Dry apricots, 300 g

Sugar, 150 g

Whole cloves, 3

Cinnamon stick, 1 cm

Small nutmeg, whole, 1/4

1. Cut apricots into halves or quarters.
2. Place all ingredients in a jar and shake.
3. Macerate for 4 weeks, shake jar twice a week.
4. Strain and filter.
5. Bottle and age for one month.

Fresh Apricot

Alcohol 60%, 500 ml

Fresh apricots, 300 g

Sugar, 150 g

Whole cloves, 3

Cinnamon stick, 1 cm

Small nutmeg, whole, 1/4

1. Cut apricots into halves or quarters. Save 25% of the pits.
2. Place all ingredients in a jar and shake.
3. Macerate for 3 weeks, shake jar twice a week.
4. Strain the infusion and filter through paper towel.
5. Bottle and age one month.

Aromatic

Alcohol 40%, 1 liter

Ginger, 1 slice (1/2 tsp. powdered ginger)

Whole cloves, 5

Nutmeg 1/3 nut

Vanilla, ½ stick (2 g)

Cinnamon, 1 cm stick

Allspice, 3 berries

Honey, 3 tablespoons

Orange skin infusion*

Lemon skin infusion**

1. Dilute honey in equal amount of warm water.

2. Place all ingredients except orange and lemon infusions in a jar and add alcohol (vodka).

3. Shake the jar and let macerate for 3 weeks. Shake the jar twice a week.

4. Strain and filter. Add 30 ml of orange and 10 ml of lemon infusions.

5. Bottle and age for one month.

Notes:

* 10 g orange skins, 50 ml 75% alcohol, macerate 3 days, strain and bottle.

** 10 g lemon skin, 50 ml 75% alcohol, macerate 3 days, strain and bottle.

Bakalia

Prunes with pits, 200 g

Raisins, 150 g

Alcohol 50%, 600 ml

Vanilla, 2 g (1/2 stick)

Almond, crushed, 1

Cinnamon stick, 1 cm

Orange skin infusion*, 15 ml (1 Tbsp.)

Honey, 30 ml

1. Remove pits. Save 25% pits and crush them.

2. Place prunes and crushed pits in a jar, add raisins, remaining ingredients and alcohol.

3. Macerate for 3 weeks.

4. Strain and filter.

5. Bottle and age for one month.

Notes:

* 10 g orange skins, 50 ml 75% alcohol, macerate 3 days, strain and bottle.

Banana

Bananas, 500 g

Alcohol 60%, 500 ml

Cloves, 2

Cinnamon, 1 cm stick

Vanilla, 2 g (1/2 stick)

Sugar syrup 73%, 250 ml

1. Peel off the skin and slice bananas.

2. Add alcohol.

3. Macerate for 4 weeks. Shake jar twice a week.

4. Strain and filter. *Store for future use (don't add sugar syrup) OR:*

5. Add sugar syrup.

6. Bottle and age for one month.

Banana-Strawberry

Bananas, 500 g

Strawberries, 500 g

Alcohol 60%, 1000 ml

Alcohol 40%, 750 ml

Cloves, 2

Cinnamon, 1 cm stick

Vanilla, 2 g (1/2 stick)

Sugar, 500 g.

1. Peel off the skin, and slice bananas. Cut strawberries into halves. Place fruit in a jar.

2. Add 1 liter of 60% alcohol.

3. Macerate for 3 weeks. Shake jar twice a week.

4. Strain, filter and bottle.

5. Add 500 g sugar to the leftover fruit.

6. Pour 750 ml of 40% alcohol into the fruit.

7. Macerate for 3 weeks. Shake jar twice a week.

8. Strain and filter.

9. Combine both infusions together.

10. Bottle and age month.

Black Tea

Black tea, 25 g

Cinnamon stick, 3 cm

Cloves (1)

Lemon skin (1 lemon)

Rum 30 ml

Alcohol 75%, 500 ml

1. Place tea with cinnamon and clove in a teapot. Pour in boiling water and cover the teapot with a towel. Let it cool and filter.

2. Place in a jar cut up lemon skin (without pith), rum, alcohol and the tea infusion. Close the lid.

3. Macerate for one week.

4. Filter and bottle.

5. Age for month.

Blueberries

Blueberries, 500 g

Alcohol 70%, 500 ml

Sugar syrup 73%, 250 ml

1. Place blueberries in a jar and crush them.

2. Add alcohol, close the lid.

3. Macerate for 4 weeks. Shake jar twice a week.

4. Strain and filter through paper towel. Add sugar syrup.

5. Bottle and age for one month.

Cherry

Cherries, 400 g

Alcohol, 70%, 500 ml

Sugar 150 g

Cloves, 2

1. Place cherries in a jar, add sugar, cloves and alcohol.

2. Macerate for 3 weeks. Shake jar twice a week.

3. Strain and filter.

4. Bottle and age for 2 months.

Chocolate Infusion

Bitter chocolate, 100 g

Vanilla stick (4 g)

Alcohol 60%, 600 ml

Orange skin (1/2 orange)

Sugar syrup 73%, 300 ml

1. Cut vanilla stick into small pieces. Break chocolate into small pieces. Place them with cut up orange skin in a jar and add alcohol.

2. Macerate for 10 days, shaking jar every day. Filter and mix with sugar syrup.

3. Bottle and age for one week.

Elderberry Infusion

Sambucus (elder or elderberry) is a genus of between 5 and 30 species of shrubs or small trees in the moschatel family. Only black elderberry, either European *Sambucus Nigra* or closely related American *Sambucus Canadensis* are suitable for culinary uses. Elderberry grows in a variety of conditions including both wet and dry soils, primarily in sunny locations. Uses for the fruit include medicinal products, wine, jelly, cordials and dye. Wine, brandies or liqueurs made from Elderberry are made by almost every European country.

Dry elderberry berries, 100 g

Alcohol 60%, 600 ml

1 lemon without skin and seeds, broken into wedges

Ginger, 5 slices

Cinnamon stick, 2 cm

Sugar, 100 g

1. Place all ingredients in a jar. Add alcohol.

2. Macerate for 3 weeks.

3. Strain and filter.

4. Bottle and age for a month.

Notes:

For fresh elderberries take: fresh elderberries 400 g, alcohol 70% 600 ml. Other ingredients and instructions as above.

Ginger Honey

Fresh ginger, 100 g

Lemon, small (2), 200 g

Honey, 200 ml (280 g)

Alcohol 70%, 500 ml

Cloves, 2

Cinnamon stick, 2 cm

1. Slice ginger. Cut lemons into wedges.

2. Place all ingredients in a jar. Add alcohol and stir.

3. Macerate for one month. Shake jar twice a week.

4. Strain and filter.

5. Bottle and age one month.

Ginger-Lemon

Fresh ginger, 100 g

Sugar, 200 g

2 lemons

Alcohol 75%, 600 ml

Water 200 ml

1. Mix water with sugar in a jar. Peel off ginger and slice. Add ginger.

2. Peel of lemon skins and separate lemons into wedges removing seeds. Add lemons (without skins) into the jar.

3. Add 500 ml of 75% alcohol and shake the jar.

4. Remove the pith under the lemon skin. Cut skins into 1 cm pieces. Place in a second glass jar and cover with 100 ml of 75% alcohol. Macerate for 3 days, strain and add the liquid into the main jar.

5. Macerate for 3 weeks and filter.

6. Bottle and one month.

Grapefruit

Grapefruit 400 g, 1

Small orange, skin only, 1

Vanilla stick, 1/2

Cinnamon stick, 1 cm

Clove 1

Sugar, 200 g

Alcohol 75%, 500 ml

1. Peel off the skin from one grapefruit. Squeeze the juice out.

2. Peel of the skin of one small orange. Slice into strips. Avoid white pith.

3. Place all ingredients in a jar and add alcohol.

4. Macerate for 2 weeks, shaking jar daily.

5. Strain and filter.

6. Bottle and age for one week.

Notes:

Both white and pink grapefruits are suitable, the pink being little sweeter. What comes as a surprise is that the filtered infusions come crystal clear.

The flavor is somewhat similar to lemon juice only weaker and more subtle. Because of that it agrees well with honey and all sweet juices.

Don't add sugar if you want to store the infusion as a raw material for future use.

Griotte

Griotte is a delicious spirit which is made from sour cherries and black currants. There is sweet Polish Griotte Vodka (38%) and Czech Griotte Liqueur (20%).

Griotte Infusion:

Sour cherries, 400 g

Black currants, 100 g

Vanilla, 2 g (1/2 stick)

Alcohol 75%, 750 ml

1. Place black currants in a jar and crush them. Discard pits from sour cherries and add sour cherries into the jar. Add vanilla and alcohol.

2. Macerate for 4 weeks. Shake jar twice a week.

3. Filter infusion. Add 200 ml of 73% sugar syrup and stir.

4. Bottle and age for one month.

Notes:

Griotte was often made with violet root (Viola odorata), about 2 g will the right amount for 1 liter infusion. Combination of vanilla and violet provides unique aroma.

Hawthorn Infusion

Hawthorn (*Crataegus monogyna*) commonly called thornapple, is a large genus of shrubs and trees in the rose family, Rosaceae, native to temperate regions of the Northern Hemisphere in Europe, Asia and North America. The fruit of hawthorn, called haws, are  edible raw but are commonly made into jellies, jams, and syrups, used to make wine, or to add flavor to brandy. Petals are also edible, as are the leaves, if picked in spring when still young, they are tender enough to be used in salads.

Hawthorn has been used in traditional medicine for centuries and is credited with lowering blood pressure, in treating chronic heart failure and helping with arrhythmia problems.

Hawthorn berries, 1000 g

Alcohol 50%, 1000 ml

3 cloves,

Cinnamon, 1 cm

Sugar syrup 73%, 50 ml

1. Cover berries with alcohol.

2. Macerate for 3 weeks.

3. Strain and filter. Add sugar syrup.

4. Bottle and age for one month.

Horseradish Infusion

Similarly to krupnik vodka this infusion will warm you up in winter time.

Horseradish, 100 g

Honey, 50 ml

Lemon juice, 10 ml (2 tsp.)

Lemon skin (1/2 lemon)

Alcohol 60%, 350 ml

1. Grate horseradish through large holes. Mix with honey and lemon juice. Add cut up lemon skin and alcohol.

2. Macerate for 4 days. Shake daily.

3. Filter and bottle.

Notes:

To make it hotter mix with ingredients ½ small cayenne pepper.

Kiwi

Kiwi produces one of the clearest infusions there is. The flavor is somewhat similar to lemon juice only much weaker and more subtle. Because of that it agrees well with honey and all sweet juices.

Kiwi, 500 g

Alcohol 60%, 500 ml

Sugar syrup 73%, 250 ml

1. Slice kiwis and place in a jar.

2. Add alcohol.

3. Macerate for 4 weeks. Shake jar twice a week. *Store for future use (don't add sugar syrup) OR:*

4. Strain and filter through paper towel. Add sugar syrup.

5. Bottle and age for one month.

Lemon-Coffee

This infusion calls for an unusual technique that makes an interesting show piece.

Alcohol 50%, 500 ml,

Medium size lemon, 1 (150 g)

Whole coffee beans, 18

Sugar, 100 g

1. Bring water to a boil, switch off the heat and immerse whole lemon for 2-3 minutes.

2. Make a series of short cuts on lemon skins all around. Place a coffee bean in each.

3. Mix sugar with an equal amount of warm water.

4. Place the lemon inside a jar, add sugar syrup and alcohol.

5. Macerate for 2-3 weeks.

6. Remove lemon, cut in half and squeeze the juice off. Strain the juice and add to infusion.

7. Filter infusion, bottle and age one month.

Linden Rose

Dry rose petals, 5 g

Dry linden flowers, 15 g

Linden honey, 300 g

Alcohol 75%, 750 ml

Water, 500 ml

1. Place rose petals and linden flower in a tea pot and cover with 500 ml boiling water. Let cool and strain.

2. Place rose/linden extract in a pot, add honey and bring to a boil. Boil 5 minutes removing any foam from the surface. Cool down and add alcohol.

3. Bottle and age for one month.

Loquat

The loquat (*Eriobotrya japonica*), is a fruit tree in the family Rosaceae, indigenous to central China. The tree grows in the whole Mediterranean basin and all over Florida. In Mexico it is known as "Nispero." Its nickname is Japanese plum or Chinese plum. Loquat fruits, growing in clusters, are oval, rounded or pear-shaped,  3–5 cm long, with a yellow or orange color. Loquat is eaten as a fresh fruit and mixes well with other fruits in fresh fruit salads or fruit cups. The fruits are also commonly used to make jam, jelly and chutney, and are delicious poached in light syrup. Loquats are also be used to make wine. Lemon or lemon zest is often paired with the wine because the fruit has very low acidity. The fruits are the sweetest when soft and orange. The flavor is a mix of peach, citrus and mild mango.

Loquats, 750 g

Alcohol 75%, 750 ml

Sugar, 250 g

Cinnamon, 1 stick

Cloves 2,

1. Discards seeds. Place loquats in a jar, cover with sugar and add alcohol.

2. Macerate for 3 weeks. Shake twice a week.

3. Strain and filter.

4. Bottle and age for one month.

Mango

Mangoes, 500 g

Alcohol 75%, 500 ml

Cloves, 2

Cinnamon, 1 cm stick

Sugar syrup 73%, 250 ml

1. Remove the skin and pits. Cut mangoes into smaller pieces.

2. Add alcohol.

3. Macerate for 4 weeks. Shake jar twice a week.

4. Strain and filter. *Store for future use (don't add sugar syrup) OR:*

5. Add sugar syrup.

6. Bottle and age for one month.

Notes:

Mango goes well with peaches, lemon and other tropical fruis.

Oriental

Dry figs, 125 g

Raisins, 125 g

Dry Dates, 50 g

Cacao powder*, 25 g

Sugar, 100 g

Lemon juice, teaspoon

Cloves, 1

Cinnamon, 2 cm

Alcohol 50%, 1.5 liter

1. Break fruit into smaller pieces and place in a jar.

2. Mix cacao powder with a cup of alcohol and pour into the jar. Add all spices and sugar.

3. Add alcohol.

4. Macerate for 4 weeks.

5. Strain and filter.

6. Bottle and age for one month.

Notes:

* instead cacao powder use 12 carob pods, when available.

Carob pods are native to Mediterranean region. The seed pod may be crushed and used as a substitute for chocolate.

Papaya Infusion

Papaya, 500 g

Alcohol 70%, 750 ml

Lemon juice, 1 lemon

Fresh ginger, 30 g

Cinnamon, ½ stick

Sugar, 250 g

1. Remove papaya seeds and the skin. Dice papaya into smaller pieces. Place in a jar. Add ginger and cinnamon.

2. Cover with sugar. Add alcohol.

3. Macerate for 3 weeks. Shake jar twice a week. Strain and filter.

4. Bottle and age one month.

Peach

Peaches, 500 g

Alcohol 75%, 500 ml

Cloves, 1

Cinnamon, 1 cm stick

Cardamom, 1 seed

Sugar syrup 73%, 250 ml

1. Save 6 pits, discard the rest. Crush saved pits, remove the seeds and place in a jar. Cut peaches into small pieces and add with cinnamon and cloves into the jar. Remove cardamom seed from a pod and add into the jar. Add alcohol.

2. Macerate for 4 weeks. Shake the jar twice a week. *Filter and store for future use (don't add sugar syrup) OR:*

3. Strain and filter. Add sugar syrup.

4. Bottle and age for one month.

Pear

Pears, 500 g

Alcohol 75%, 500 ml

Vanilla stick, 1/2

Cloves, 2

Cinnamon, 1 cm stick

Ginger, 1 slice

Sugar syrup 73%, 250 ml

1. Place pears in a jar and crush them.

2. Add alcohol, close the lid.

3. Macerate for 4 weeks. Shake jar twice a week. *Filter and store for future use (don't add sugar syrup) OR:*

4. Strain and filter. Add sugar syrup.

5. Bottle and age for one month.

Pharmacist

This is another original Polish classic known as "Farmaceutow" which means *Pharmacists Infusion*. It is made of alcohol, milk and lemon juice, and obviously it breaks immediately down creating a kind of cheese. After aging, it is filtered and very good.

300 g lemons

300 g full milk (3.2%)

400 ml 75% alcohol.

½ (1.5 g) vanilla stick

2 cloves

1. Peel off lemons, discard skins, cut lemons into rounds, remove white membranes and pits. Take the skin from one lemon, remove pith, cut up into smaller pieces and add to lemons.

2. Place into a jar, add milk, alcohol and spices.

3. Stir and macerate for one month. Shake every few days.

4. Siphon off the clear liquid from the top and filter the rest through coffee filter. Combine the clear liquid with filtered infusion and filter again.

5. For storing over a month keep in refrigerator.

Pineapple

Pineapple infusion has such a wonderful and characteristic aroma that it does not need help from other ingredients.

Pineapple, 300 g

Alcohol 70%, 500 ml

Sugar 150 g,

1. Peel off the skin and dice pineapple into 1 cm chunks.

2. Place fruit in a jar, add sugar syrup, add alcohol. Shake the jar.

3. Macerate for 3 weeks, shake every few days.

4. Strain and filter.

5. Bottle and age for one month.

Plum

Damson plums, 500 g

Sugar 250 g

Alcohol 70%, 750 ml

1. Discard pits, cut plums into small pieces, place in a jar and add alcohol.

2. Macerate for 4 weeks. Filter.

3. Dissolve 250 g of sugar in 250 ml of warm eater. Let it cool.

4. Add syrup to infusion and rest for 2 days.

5. Filter and bottle.

6. Age for two month.

Notes:

If it is hard to find damson plums use other variety.

Prune

Prunes with pits, 300 g

Alcohol 50%, 750 ml

Vanilla, 2 g (1/2 stick)

Almond, crushed, 1

Cinnamon stick, 1 cm

1. Remove pits. Save 25% pits and crush them.

2. Place prunes and crushed pits in a jar, add remaining ingredients and alcohol.

3. Macerate for 3 weeks.

4. Filter and bottle.

5. Age one month.

Quince

Quince (*Cydonia oblonga*) is hard, astringent and sour to eat fruit. High in pectin, they are used to make jam, jelly and quince pudding. Adding a diced quince to apple sauce will enhance the taste of the apple sauce with the chunks of relatively firm, tart quince. The term "marmalade", originally meaning a quince jam, comes from "marmelo," the Portuguese word for this fruit.

Quince infusion

Quinces, 500 g

Alcohol 60%, 500 ml

Cloves, 2

Cinnamon, 1 cm stick

Sugar syrup 73%, 250 ml

1. Remove the skin, pits and cut fruit into smaller pieces.

2. Add alcohol.

3. Macerate for 4 weeks. Shake jar twice a week. *Store for future use (don't add sugar syrup) OR:*

4. Strain and filter through paper towel. Add sugar syrup.

5. Bottle and age for one month.

Raspberry

Raspberries, 300 g

Alcohol, 70%, 500 ml

Sugar syrup 150 ml

1 lime

1. Place raspberries in a jar and add alcohol.

2. Macerate for 3 weeks. Shake jar twice a week.

3. Strain.

Save fruit for the second infusion (optional)*

4. Add sugar syrup and stir well. Add filtered juice from ½ lime.

5. Bottle and age for 2 months.

The second infusion:

Continue after step 3

300 ml 60% alcohol

1. Cover leftover fruit with 150 g sugar and add 60% alcohol. Add ½ lime. Stir.

2. Macerate for 3 weeks. Shake jar twice a week.

3. Strain, filter and bottle.

Notes:

Raspberry juice is very sweet. Infusion will benefit from adding citric acid at about 0.5 g per one liter. In this recipes lime juice is used.

Strawberry Ratafia

Although ratafias are easy to make, nevertheless they have very sophisticated composition which is the sum of each fruit involved.

Strawberries, 250 g

Banana, 250 g

Kiwi, 250 g

Sugar, 375 g

Alcohol 70%, 750 ml

Part I

1. Place strawberries in a jar, cover with 125 g of sugar, pour in 250 ml of alcohol.

2. Place bananas in a jar, cover with 125 g of sugar, pour in 250 ml of alcohol.

3. Place kiwis in a jar, cover with 125 g of sugar, pour in 250 ml of alcohol.

4. Macerate for 4 weeks. Shake the jar twice a week.

5. Strain, filter and bottle. This is your best quality 1st infusion.

Part II

1. Place leftover fruit in a jar, add 100 g sugar and 500 ml of 40% alcohol.

2. Macerate for 3 weeks, shake the jar twice a week.

3. Strain, filter and bottle. This is your 2nd infusion.

Notes:

Taste your 1st infusion. Decide whether you want any changes made to the second infusion. You can add a slice or two of ginger, cinnamon, cloves, vanilla or other ingredients. This way your second infusion will have a different character.

Both infusions can be kept as separate drinks or they may be combined together.

Ratafia –Tutti-Frutti

This is a fun project. Assuming that you live in the climate where the winter is part of the year, start making infusion in March. Get the biggest jar or suitable container available. Every time new fruit shows in the supermarket, buy it and add it to your collection. You should be done in November.

Tutti-Frutti Traditional

Part I

1. Place strawberries in a jar, cover with sugar, then cover with 75% alcohol.

2. Place bananas in a jar, cover with sugar, then cover with 75% alcohol.

3. Place kiwi in a jar, cover with sugar, then cover with 75% alcohol.

Continue adding other fruit (apples, pears, plums, cherries) when available. When adding oranges, discard the skin and seeds. You can use dry fruit as well.

4. Once the container is full, let it macerate one more month.

5. Strain, filter and bottle. This is your best quality 1st infusion.

Part II

1. Place leftover fruit in a container, add little sugar and cover with 40% alcohol.

2. Macerate for 3 weeks, shake container twice a week.

3. Strain, filter and bottle. This is your 2nd infusion.

Notes:

Taste your 1st infusion. Decide whether you want any changes made to the second infusion. You can add a slice or two of ginger, cinnamon, cloves, vanilla or other ingredients. This way your second infusion will have a different character. Both infusions can be kept as separate drinks or they may be combined together.

Options:

You can go with a more scientific approach, but that takes all the fun away. The rule of a thumb dictates that: for each 100 g of fruit, add 100 ml of 75% alcohol and 50 g of sugar. It is impossible to predict which version will be better.

The most scientific approach is to use only fruit and alcohol, eg. 100 g fruit and 100 ml 75% alcohol. Then once ratafia is strained and filtered, measure its volume and decide how much sugar syrup it needs. Taste first. You can also harmonize its flavor by adding spices, citrus acid or adding more alcohol.

However, nothing beats the fun of doing it by ear and testing once a while.

Sour Cherry

Sour cherries, 400 g

Alcohol, 70%, 500 ml

Vanilla, 2 g (1/2 stick)

Cloves, 2

Cinnamon, 1 cm

Sugar syrup 73%, 120 ml (120 g sugar)

1. Place sour cherries in a jar. Add spices and alcohol.

2. Macerate for 4 weeks. Shake twice a week.

3. Strain and filter. Straining may be enough as sour cherries produce very clean juice.

Store for later use, for example to make combination fruit vodka OR

4. Add sugar syrup and stir well.

5. Bottle and age for 1-2 days. The final product is sour cherries infusion or sour cherries vodka, whatever you want to call it.

Sour Cherry Syrup and Infusion

Sour cherries are the excellent juice producer. In addition, the juice is very clear and in most cases the straining is all that is needed. Sour cherries syrup is wonderful and full of aroma, much better than strawberry syrup. The only syrup that can compete with it is raspberry syrup.

Sour cherries syrup:

Sour cherries 1 kg, save 20% pits

Sugar, 1 kg

1. Remove pits, save 20% pits, discard the rest. Place sour cherries and pits (uncrushed) in a glass jar.

2. Cover with sugar but don't mix. Close the container tight.

3. Macerate for 10 days. Shake the jar every few days. Mix well and strain into a cooking pot. Save the fruit for infusion. The syrup should not occupy more than a half of the volume of the pot.

4. Bring to a boil, switch off the heat and scoop up any foam from the top. Let it cool.

5. Pour into bottles. Use for any general purposes.

Sour cherries infusion:

Leftover sour cherries

60% alcohol, 750 ml

1. Add alcohol to leftover sour cherries, mix and macerate for 4 weeks. Shake the jar twice a week.

2. Strain, filter and bottle.

Notes:

Estimated alcohol content around 30%. Add 250 ml of 75% alcohol if you like strong drinks.

Strawberry

Strawberries, 400 g

Alcohol, 70%, 500 ml

Sugar, 100 g

Lemon juice, 1 lemon

1. Place strawberries in a jar and cover with sugar. Rest for 2 hours.

2. Add lemon juice and alcohol.

3. Macerate for 3 weeks. Shake gently the jar twice a week.

4. Strain and filter.

5. Bottle and age for 2 months.

Tropical

Banana, 2

Pineapple, 2 slices

Small lemon (without skin), ½

Honey, 200 g

Water, 200 ml

Alcohol 40%, 1000 ml

Star anise, 1

Cloves, 3

Cinnamon stick, 5 cm

Nutmeg powder, 1/3 tsp.

Vanilla stick (3 g) or vanilla infusion*, 30 ml

1. Remove the skin and dice banana and pineapple. Peel off the skin and break lemon into wedges, remove seeds.

2. Place all fruits in a jar and add all spices.

3. Mix honey with water and pour into the jar.

4. Add alcohol and stir all.

5. Macerate 4 weeks, shake jar twice a week.

6. Strain and filter.

7. Bottle and age for one month.

Notes:

*10 g vanilla stick, 90 ml alcohol 50%, macerate 3 weeks, filter and bottle.

Vodkas

Apricot Vodka

Apricot Infusion:

Fresh apricots, 500 g

Alcohol 70%, 500 ml

Whole cloves, 3

Cinnamon stick, 1 cm

Small nutmeg, whole, 1/4

1. Cut apricots into halves or quarters. Save 25% of the pits. Crush pits.

2. Place all ingredients in a jar and stir.

3. Macerate for 3 weeks, shake jar twice a week.

4. Strain and filter.

Apricot Vodka:

Apricot infusion, 300 ml

Sugar syrup 73%, 200 ml

Alcohol 75%, 500 ml

1. Mix infusion with sugar syrup.

2. Add alcohol.

3. Bottle and age for one month.

Bison Grass Vodka

Bison Grass Vodka has been one of the bestselling Polish vodkas (*Zubrowka*) for many years. The vodka is of a very light green color, having a distinct flavor and contains a long blade of bison grass inside. *Hierochloe odorata* also known as sweet grass, buffalo grass, bison grass, holy grass (UK), manna grass, Mary's grass, seneca grass, sweetgrass, or vanilla grass, is an aromatic herb which grows in northern Eurasia and in North America. It owes its distinctive sweet scent to the presence of coumarin.

The infusion is made from 0.1-0.2 g (0.1-0.2%) bison grass and 1 liter of 40% vodka with around 1% sugar (10 g).

Bison Grass Vodka

Vodka, 40%, 1 liter

Dry bison grass, 1 g (about 6 eight inch long blades of grass)

OR 1 ml 60% infusion (1 g grass, 9 ml 60% alcohol, 3 weeks)

Sugar, 5 g (1 teaspoon)

1. Mix all ingredients together.

2. Macerate for 3 weeks.

3. Filter and pour into bottles. Leave one single blade of grass in each bottle for decoration.

Blackthorn Vodka

Blackthorn or sloe (*Prunus spinosa*) is a species of Prunus native to Europe, western Asia, and locally in northwest Africa, New Zealand and eastern North America. The fruit is similar to a small damson plum, suitable for preserves, but rather tart and astringent for eating. Being a plum, blackthorn makes great wine, jam and stronger spirits. Like rowan, the fruit matures in the fall and should be picked up after first freeze. Infusion can be made from freshly harvested or dry fruit. It is similar to rowan berries and often a small amount of dogwood infusion is added to rowan vodka.

Blackthorn infusion:

150 g dry blackthorn berries

50% alcohol, 750 ml

10 g sugar

1. Pour alcohol over berries and macerate for 3 weeks. Shake the jar twice a week.

2. Strain, add sugar and bottle.

Blackthorn vodka:

Take 500 ml infusion. Infusion is vodka.

Small amounts of blackthorn infusion are often added to other spirits, for example rowan or dogwood vodkas.

Candy Vodka

Clear hard candies produce very clear vodkas. Pick your favored candy and make vodka out of it.

Alcohol 40% (vodka), 500 ml

Clear hard candy, 50 g

1. Select the type of candy that you like. Red candy will produce red vodka and a green colored one will produce green colored vodka.

2. Place vodka and candy in a glass jar, cover and shake. Periodically shake the jar until all candy will dissolve in vodka.

3. Filter through a funnel lined up with paper towel or coffee filter.

4. Bottle.

Notes:

Increasing the amount of candy will result in sweeter vodka.

Jolly Rancher® candies are exceptionally clear and come in wonderful flavors.

Caraway Vodka

You love caraway or you hate it. It goes into rye bread, sauerkraut, pickles, Allasch liqueur and other spirits.

Caraway Vodka, 500 ml:

Caraway infusion*, 125 ml

Star anise infusion**, 5 ml

Lemon skin infusion***, 10 ml

Sugar syrup 73%, 25 ml
Alcohol 75%, 250 ml
Water, 85 ml

1. Mix infusions with water, then mix with sugar syrup.
2. Keep on mixing and start slowly adding alcohol.
3. Bottle and age for one month.

Notes:

Caraway infusion: 25 g caraway, 250 ml 50% alcohol, 3 weeks.
Star anise infusion: 10 g anise, 50 ml 50% alcohol, 3 weeks.
Lemon skins infusion: 10 g skins, 50 ml 75% alcohol, 3-4 days maceration time.

Cayenne Vodka, 500 ml

Vodka 40%, 500 ml
Black peppercorns, 10
½ small red cayenne pepper
Fresh ginger, 1 slice

1. Throw peppercorns, cayenne and ginger into the bottle of vodka.
2. Macerate for 2 weeks, shake the bottle twice a week.
3. Strain and filter.
4. Add 1 teaspoon of sugar.
5. Add a few drops of caramel for color.
6. Age one day.

Cranberry Vodka

Cranberry Infusion:

Dry cranberries, 200 g

Alcohol 50%, 1000 ml

Cloves, 2

Cinnamon, 2cm

Nutmeg, ¼ nut

Ginger, 3 slices

1. Mix everything together with alcohol.

2. Macerate for 3 weeks. Strain and filter. This is your first infusion which you can keep for blending spirits. Cranberry goes well with anything that is sweet such as honey, strawberry or raspberry.

Cranberry Vodka:

Cranberry infusion, 400 ml.

Sugar syrup, 100 ml

1. Mix cranberry infusion with sugar syrup.

2. Bottle and age one week.

3. Optional step: Add 200 g of sugar and 500 ml of 40% alcohol to leftover fruit, macerate for 3 weeks. Strain, filter and bottle. This is your second infusion.

Notes:

Dry cranberries are sweetened. Taste infusion for sweetness before adding sugar syrup.

If fresh cranberries are used make infusion as: 750 g cranberries, 750 ml 50% alcohol. Spices as above. More sugar syrup is needed (200 – 300 g/l), unless dry vodka is preferred.

Dogwood Vodka

Dogwood vodka has the opinion as the one of the finest fruit vodkas there is.

The European Cornel (Cornus mas), Cornelian Cherry, is a species of dogwood native to southern Europe, Armenia, Iran and southwest Asia. In North America, the plant is known by the common name of Cornelian Cherry. It has an acidic flavor which is best described as a mixture of cranberry and sour cherry; it makes great jam sauce and vodka. There are many species of dogwood plant in the USA, *Cornus canadensis* being very similar.

From Wikipedia: The berries when ripe on the plant bear a resemblance to coffee berries, and ripen in mid to late summer. The fruit is edible (mainly in Iran), but the unripe fruit is astringent. The fruit only fully ripens after it falls from the tree. When ripe, the fruit is dark ruby red. It has an acidic flavor which is best described as a mixture of cranberry and sour cherry; it is mainly used for making jam, makes an excellent sauce similar to cranberry sauce when pitted and then boiled with sugar and orange, but also can be eaten dried. In the Republic of Azerbaijan and Armenia, the fruit is used for distilling vodka, while in Albania it is distilled into raki. In Poland it is called *deren* and often chosen to make outstanding infusions and vodkas.

Dogwood infusion:

200 g dry dogwood berries

50% alcohol, 1000 ml

10 g sugar

1. Pour alcohol over berries and macerate for 3 weeks. Shake the jar twice a week.

2. Strain, add sugar and bottle.

Making vodka:

1. Take 500 ml infusion. Infusion is vodka.

Grapefruit Vodka

Grapefruit (skinned), 500 g
Alcohol 75%, 500 ml
Sugar, 10 g

1. Peel the skin off and remove white pith from the fruit. Squeeze the juice out.
2. Macerate with alcohol for two weeks.
3. Strain and filter. Add sugar.
4. Bottle and age one week.

Notes:

White or pink grapefruit is suitable. Filtered infusion is crystal clear.

Juniper Vodka, 500 ml

Well known juniper flavored spirit is gin which is made by distilling juniper infusion. At home, juniper vodka can substitute for gin and it can be easily made by macerating dry juniper berries with alcohol.

Alcohol 40%, 500 ml
Juniper berries, 0.5 g (12 dry berries)
Sugar, 2 g (1/2 tsp.)
Ginger, 1 slice
Dry lemon skin, 2 strips

1. Add berries, ginger and dry lemon skin to a bottle of vodka.
2. Macerate for 3 weeks, shaking bottle every two days.
3. Strain, add sugar and pour into bottles.
4. Age for one day.

Kiwi Vodka

Kiwi, 500 g

Alcohol 60%, 750 ml

1. Slice kiwis and place in a jar.

2. Add alcohol.

3. Macerate for 3 weeks. Shake jar twice a week.

4. Filter infusion. Taste and add sugar syrup if you like sweet vodkas.

5. Bottle and age for two days.

Notes:

Kiwi infusion is vodka.

Unsweetened kiwi infusion is a great material for blending with other juices.

Krupnik

Krupnik is a classical Polish vodka made with honey. Aromatic spices, in combination with honey give Krupnik its unique flavor. Due to the high proportion of honey Krupnik can be considered to be the honey liqueur.

Honey, 350 ml

Alcohol 75%, 600 ml

Aromatic infusions* 30 ml total,

Caramel syrup (optional), 5 ml

Citric acid, 1.5 g or 1 tsp. lemon juice

Water to 1 liter mark

Instructions:

1. Add water to honey and bring to boil. Remove any foam that forms on the surface. Add spices.

2. Remove from heat, keep on stirring and add alcohol.

3. Pour into bottles. You may serve Krupnik the moment it is done, but its taste improves in time.

Notes:

*Aromatic infusions: vanilla, ginger, cinnamon, cloves, nutmeg, lemon skins.

In winter Krupnik was often served hot.

Krupnik - Raspberry

Krupnik is a classical Polish vodka made with honey. Aromatic spices, in combination with honey give Krupnik its unique flavor. Due to the high proportion of honey Krupnik can be considered to be the honey liqueur. Krupnik often includes raspberry or sour cherry infusions.

Honey, 300 ml

Raspberry infusion**, 100 ml

Alcohol 75%, 500 ml

Aromatic infusions* 30 ml total,

Citric acid, 1.5 g or 1 tsp. lemon juice

Water to 1 liter mark

Instructions:

1. Mix honey with water, add raspberry infusion and bring to boil. Scoop up any foam. Add spices.

2. Remove from heat, keep on stirring and add alcohol.

3. Pour into bottles.

Notes:

*Aromatic infusions: vanilla, ginger, cinnamon, cloves, nutmeg.

**Raspberry infusion: raspberries, 150 g, alcohol, 70%, 250 ml, macerate for 3 weeks, strain.

Kumquat Vodka

Kumquats are the small yellow to orange citrus fruits being approximately the size and shape of an olive with sweet spongy rind and somewhat acid pulp that are used chiefly for preserves, marmalade, and jelly.

Single orange and Kumquats.

Kumquat Infusion:

Kumquats, 1.5 kg
70% alcohol, 1.5 liter
Vanilla 10 g, (2 stick)
Crushed almonds, 20
Cloves, 5

1. Remove seeds by squeezing them out from the fruit. Add almonds, vanilla and cloves.

2. Add alcohol.

3. Macerate for 3 weeks. Shake jar twice a week.

4. Strain and filter.

Kumquat Vodka:

Kumquat infusion, 500 ml
Sugar syrup 73%, 300 ml
Lemon skin extract/infusion*, 15 ml
Alcohol 75%, 200 ml

1. Mix infusions together.

2. Add sugar syrup.

3. Add alcohol.

4. Bottle and age one month.

Notes:

* Lemon skins, 10 g, alcohol 75%, 50 ml, 4 days.

Lemon Vodka

Lemon vodka is one of the finest vodkas that can be made.

Alcohol 75%	500 ml
Lemon skin infusion*,	100 ml
Orange skin infusion*,	20 ml
Ginger infusion**	50 ml
Sugar syrup 73%	200 ml
Citric acid,	2.0 g
Saffron for color, just a touch (1/10 tsp)	
Water,	100 ml

1. Measure 100 ml of water and add 1/10 teaspoon of saffron. The solution will develop the real lemon skin color within minutes. Strain.

2. Mix alcohol with lemon, orange and ginger infusion. Add citric acid and stir.

3. Place sugar syrup in a different jar.

4. Keep on stirring syrup and start slowly adding mixture of alcohol infusions.

5. Place the solution in a measuring jar and add saffron water.

6. Stir the contents and add water to 1 liter mark.

7. Bottle and age for one week.

Notes:

*100 g fresh orange/lemon skins without white pith, macerated for 3-4 days in 500 ml 70% alcohol. Strain after maceration. Add as needed.

** fresh cut up ginger, 100 g, 50% alcohol 100 ml, macerate 3 weeks, strain and filter.

Fresh lemon juice may be added in place of citric acid (about 30 ml, two tablespoons), however vodka's clarity will suffer.

Mandarin Vodka, 500 ml

Save orange skins when making fresh orange juice. Remove the white pith, cut skins into long strips and dry them out. Then, place in the air tight container. Dry orange skins are full of aroma and store exceptionally well.

Mandarin orange skins
(5 mandarines), 50 g

Sugar syrup (73%), 150 ml (200 g)

Alcohol 75%, 250 ml

Water, 50 ml

1. Place dry orange skins in a jar, add alcohol and macerate for 3-4 days.

2. Filter and combine with sugar syrup. Add water.

3. Bottle and age for a week.

Mint Candy Vodka

Ice blue mint candies produce light blue vodkas with a refreshing mint flavor. There are many mint candies on the market, the two which are well known are Blue Peppermint Candy by Atkinson's® and Ice Blue Mint Coolers® by Brach's®.

Alcohol 40% (vodka), 500 ml

Clear mint candy, 50 g

1. Select the type of mint candy that you like.

2. Place vodka and candy in a glass jar, cover and shake. Periodically shake the jar until all candy will dissolve in vodka.

3. Filter through a funnel lined up with paper towel or coffee filter.

4. Bottle.

Notes:

Increasing the amount of candy will result in sweeter vodka.

Orange Vodka - Dry

Orange infusion*, 400 ml

Orange skin infusion**, 30 ml

Lemon skins infusion***, 10 ml (2 tsp.)

Alcohol 75%, 350 ml

Sugar syrup (73%), 50 ml

Water to 1 liter mark (about 50 ml)

1. Mix orange and lemon skins infusions with 350 ml of 75% alcohol. Add orange infusion*.

2. Mix infusions with sugar syrup.

3. Bottle and age one week.

Notes:

*200 g orange (no skin), 250 ml 75% alcohol, 2 cloves, 3 ginger slices. Remove the skins and save for making orange skin infusion. Divide oranges into wedges, remove seeds and crush the fruit. Add cloves, ginger and alcohol. Macerate for 3 weeks. Strain and filter.

**10 g fresh orange skins without white pith, macerated for 3-4 days in 50 ml 75% alcohol. Strain and bottle.

***10 g fresh lemon skins without white pith, macerated for 3-4 days in 50 ml 75% alcohol. Strain after maceration.

Orange Vodka – Sweet

Orange infusion*, 400 ml

Orange skin infusion**, 40 ml

Lemon skins infusion***, 15 ml (2 tsp.)

Alcohol 75%, 250 ml

Sugar syrup 73%, 300 ml

1. Mix orange and lemon skins infusions with 350 ml of 75% alcohol. Add orange infusion*.

2. Mix infusions with sugar syrup.

3. Bottle and age one week.

Notes:

*200 g orange (no skin), 250 ml 75% alcohol, 3 cloves, 3 ginger slice, 1 cm cinnamon stick. Remove the skins and save for making orange skin infusion. Divide oranges into wedges, remove seeds and crush the fruit. Add cloves, ginger and alcohol. Macerate for 3 weeks. Strain and filter.

**10 g fresh orange skins without white pith, macerated for 3-4 days in 50 ml 75% alcohol. Strain and bottle.

***10 g fresh lemon skins without white pith, macerated for 3-4 days in 50 ml 75% alcohol. Strain after maceration.

Pepper Vodka, 500 ml

This is such a simple vodka to make that there is no need to make infusion.

Vodka 40%, 500 ml
Black peppercorns, 12
Lemon skins infusion*, 5 ml

1. Throw peppercorns into the bottle of vodka.
2. Macerate for 2 weeks, shake the bottle twice a week.
3. Strain and filter.
4. Add 1 teaspoon of sugar and lemon skins infusion.
5. Add a few drops of caramel for color.
6. Age one day.

Notes:

* 10 g lemon skins, 50 ml 75% alcohol, macerate for 3 days, strain.

Peppermint Vodka

Peppermint Infusion:

Dry peppermint, 50 g
Alcohol 50%, 750 ml
Macerate for 3 weeks. Filter and bottle.

Peppermint Vodka:

Peppermint infusion, 400 ml
Sugar syrup 73%, 100 ml
Alcohol 40%, 500 ml
Citric acid, 0.3 g (3 ml, 10% solution)

1. Mix peppermint infusion with sugar syrup and citric acid.
2. Add alcohol, bottle and age for one day.

Peppermint - Herbal Vodka

Peppermint Herbal Infusion:

Dry peppermint, 50 g

Star anise, 2 stars

Cardamom, 1 pod (seeds only)

Alcohol 50%, 750 ml

Macerate for 3 weeks. Strain and filter.

Peppermint Herbal Vodka:

Peppermint herbal infusion, 400 ml

Orange skins infusion*, 15 ml

Sugar syrup 73%, 150 ml

Alcohol 75%, 250 ml

Water, 200 ml

1. Mix peppermint infusion with sugar syrup.

2. Mix orange skins infusion with 75% alcohol.

3. Combine both infusions.

4. Add water.

Notes:

* 10 g orange skins (without pith), 50 ml 75% alcohol, macerate 3 days, strain and bottle.

Plum Vodka

Damson plums make the best infusions and slivovitz brandy, but you may use any plums you can find.

Plum infusion:

Plums, 1 kg

70% alcohol, 1 liter

Vanilla 4 g, (1 stick)

Crushed almonds, 10

Cloves, 2

1. Remove pits and cut plums into smaller pieces. Add almonds, vanilla and cloves.

2. Add alcohol.

3. Macerate for 3 weeks. Shake jar twice a week.

4. Strain and filter.

Plum vodka:

Plum infusion, 500 ml

Sugar syrup 73%, 300 ml

Lemon skin extract/infusion*, 15 ml

Alcohol 75%, 200 ml

1. Mix infusions together.

2. Add sugar syrup.

3. Add alcohol.

4. Bottle and age one month.

Notes:

* Lemon skins, 10 g, alcohol 75%, 50 ml, 4 day

Porter Vodka

Very popular and original semi-sweet vodka, yet so simple to make. The main ingredient is porter dark beer, sugar, vanilla and alcohol. Many professional combine two dark beers together:

- Porter, 9.5%
- Regular dark beer 5.6%. This beer is smoother and sweeter.

Porter beer, 250 ml

Dark beer, 250 ml

Honey, 100 ml (142 g)

Alcohol 75%, 400 ml

Vanilla infusion*, 50%, 10 ml (or 1 g, 1/3 stick)

Lemon juice, 15 ml (1 tablespoon)

1. Mix both beers with honey and bring to a boil. Scoop any foam.

2. Remove from heat, add lemon juice, vanilla and alcohol.

3. Pour into bottles.

4. Age at least one day.

Notes:

* 10 g vanilla sticks, 90 ml 50% alcohol. Macerate for 3 weeks. Strain and bottle.

Honey may be replaced with sugar, although quality will slightly suffer.

Prunela

Prunes (dry plums) with pits, 300 g

Alcohol 50%, 750 ml

Vanilla, 2 g (1/2 stick)

Almond, crushed, 1

Cinnamon stick, 1 cm

1. Remove pits. Save 25% pits and crush them.

2. Place prunes and crushed pits in a jar, add remaining ingredients and alcohol.

3. Macerate for 3 weeks.

4. Filter and bottle.

5. Age for one month.

Rowan Vodka

This is a very popular in Polish dry vodka (*Jarzebiak*). Rowan is a very pretty tree with red clusters of small and tart berries. They are native throughout the cool temperate regions of the Northern Hemisphere, in the Canadian provinces of Newfoundland and Labrador and Nova Scotia this species is commonly referred to as a "Dogberry" tree. The best-known species is the European Rowan *Sorbus aucuparia*, North American native species in this subgenus include the American mountain-ash *Sorbus Americana*. The fruit matures late in the fall and the conventional wisdom says that the fruit is best when harvested after first freeze. This is a classic infusion of dry berries that results in a pretty red color and a wonderful dry flavor.

Rowan Infusion:

125 g dry rowan berries
60% alcohol, 750 ml
Sugar, 5 g (1 tsp.)

1. Pour alcohol over berries and macerate for 3 weeks. Shake the jar twice a week.
2. Strain, add sugar and bottle.

Rowan Vodka:

The rowan infusion is rowan vodka.

Notes:

This is a wonderfully tasting dry vodka of red color and superb clarity. Adding other ingredients distorts its unique flavor.

Ingredients which are occasionally added into infusion are:

Small amount of blackthorn, prunes, raisins, figs or dates.

Skittles Candy Vodka

Skittles® is a brand of fruit-flavored sweets, currently produced and marketed by the Wm. Wrigley Jr. Company, a division of Mars, Inc. Skittles® is the most popular candy among youths and the second most popular chewy candy, after Starburst, among all persons in the  United States. Skittles® can be found all over the world. A candy bag usually contains 5 different flavors of Skittles® candy and each one is of a different color.

Alcohol 40% (vodka), 500 ml

Skittles® candy, 50 g

1. Select the type of Skittle® candy that you need. Red candy will produce red vodka and green colored one will produce green colored vodka.

2. Place vodka and Skittles® candy in a glass jar, cover and shake. Periodically shake the jar until all candy will dissolve in vodka.

3. Filter through a funnel lined with paper towels or a coffee filter.

4. Bottle.

Notes:

Increasing the amount of candy will result in sweeter vodka.

Sour Cherries Vodka

Sour Cherry Infusion:

Sour cherries, 400 g

Alcohol, 75%, 500 ml

Vanilla, 2 g (1/2 stick)

Cloves, 2

Cinnamon, 1 cm

1. Break sour cherries and discard pits. Save 25% pits. Place sour cherries in a jar, including 25% uncrushed pits. Add spices and alcohol.

2. Macerate for 3 weeks. Shake the jar twice a week.

3. Strain and filter. Sour cherries produce very clean juice.

Sour Cherry Vodka:

Sour cherries infusion, 300 ml

Sugar syrup 73%, 200 ml

Alcohol 40%, 500 ml

1. Combine alcohol with sour cherry infusion.

2. Stir syrup and start slowly adding the above solution.

3. Bottle and age for 1-2 days.

Sour Cherry - Ratafia

Sour cherries vodka is a very popular household drink in Poland. Sour cherries grow everywhere, they taste delicious when mixed with sugar and they produce very clean juice. The pits, usually supplied at 25% of the total fruit weight, provide a subtle almond flavor. Often other fruit infusions are added like blueberry and raspberry. However, they should be added in small quantities at around 1-5% otherwise sour cherries will lose their dominant flavor.

Alcohol 75%, 700 ml

Sour cherries, 600 g

Raspberry, 50 g

Blueberries, 70 g

Vanilla infusion*, 60 ml (6 g vanilla sticks)

Sugar 100 g

1. Mix fruits together.

2. Add sugar and stir.

3. Add alcohol. Macerate for 3 weeks.

4. Bottle and age for one month. This is Sour Cherry Ratafia Vodka.

Notes:

* 10 g vanilla sticks, 90 ml 50% alcohol, macerate for 3 weeks. Strain and bottle.

Second Infusion - Optional

Taste your 1st infusion. Decide whether you want any changes made to the second infusion. You can add a slice or two of ginger, cinnamon, cloves, vanilla or other ingredients. This way your second infusion will have a different character. Both infusions can be kept as separate drinks or they may be combined together.

1. Place leftover fruit in a container, add 100 g sugar and cover with 40% alcohol.

2. Macerate for 3 weeks, shake container twice a week.

3. Strain, filter and bottle. This is your 2nd infusion.

Vermouth Vodka

The name "vermouth" comes from the German word Wermut for wormwood that has been used as an ingredient in the drink over its history. Wines containing wormwood as a principal ingredient existed in Germany in the 16th century. By the mid-17th century, the drink was popular in England under the name "vermouth" which has been the common name for the beverage until the present day.

Vermouth Infusion:

Cloves, 1 g
Cinnamon, 2 g
Cardamom, 2 g
Marjoram, 2 g
Coriander, 4 g
Juniper, 1 g
Chamomile, 4 g
Ginger, 2 g
Dry lemon skins, 6 g
Dry orange skins, 8 g
Wormwood, 2 g
Alcohol 50%, 500 ml

1. Place all ingredients in a jar and add alcohol.

2. Macerate for 2 weeks, strain, filter and bottle.

Vermouth Vodka:

White table wine, 300 ml

Herbal infusion, 50 ml

Sugar syrup 73%, 150 ml

Alcohol 75%, 500 ml

1. Mix wine, herbal infusion and sugar syrup. Add alcohol and stir.

2. Bottle and age 2 months.

Notes: the easiest way to make vermouth vodka is to buy a known brand vermouth wine and add little wormwood infusion. Add 5-10% sugar to dry vermouth.

Walnut Vodka

Walnut vodka is without doubt the favorite vodka made in Polish households. In Italy it is known as Nocino. Both Nocino and Polish walnut vodkas or liqueurs are typically 40% alcohol by volume, or 80 proof. The popularity of green walnut spirits can be attributed to many reasons:

- They taste good.
- Walnut trees grow everywhere.
- For centuries walnut vodka has been credited with many medicinal properties.
- They can be made as semi-sweet vodka, sweet vodka or nut liqueur.

Infusion is made from green immature walnuts which are usually picked in the last week of June. The nuts must still be soft enough to be cut with a knife into smaller pieces. Some say that a toothpick should go through the nut without difficulty.

The infusion immediately develops a light green color which becomes dark green and finally dark brown. Properly made vodka should have a distinct and pleasant nutty flavor. In the beginning the infusion may taste slightly bitter, but the flavor will improve as the infusion ages. The infusion should macerate for at least 2 months and then it can be filtered. Filtered vodka should age for at least 2 months before it is bottled. The flavor of this vodka improves and mellows in time. Spices such as ginger, cloves, nutmeg, sweet flag or angelica are often added.

Walnut Infusion:

150 g walnuts

750 ml 60% alcohol

1 clove

1 cm cinnamon

1. Cut green walnuts into smaller pieces and cover with alcohol.

2. Macerate for 4 weeks. Shake jar twice a week.

3. Strain and bottle for later use.

Walnut Vodka:

Walnut infusion, 400 ml

Sugar syrup 73%, 200 ml

Alcohol 75%, 300 ml

Water, 100 ml

1. Mix walnut infusion with sugar syrup.

2. Stirring, start slowly adding alcohol. Add 100 ml of water.

3. Bottle and age for 2 months.

Wormwood Vodka

Wormwood vodka is a bitter type of vodka. Wormwood (*Artemisia absinthium*) is the ingredient of most bitter vodkas and liqueurs, as well as herb liqueurs such as Chartreuse and Benedictine.

Wormwood Infusion:

Dry wormwood 10 g, 100 ml 50% alcohol, macerate 2 weeks. Strain and filter.

Wormwood Vodka:

Wormwood infusion, 30 ml

Sugar syrup 73%, 250 ml (250 g)

Alcohol 75%, 500 ml

Water, as needed (about 200 ml)

1. Mix 30 ml of wormwood infusion with sugar syrup.

2. Keep on stirring and slowly add alcohol.

3. Bottle and age for one month.

Liqueurs

Allasch Liqueur

Alasch was first produced in Latvia in 1823. In 1830 it was displayed in Leipzig Trade Fair, Germany and it became popular ever since. It is yellow, caraway based 30-40% strong liqueur that usually contains almonds, anise, orange skins and angelica root (*Angelica archangelica*). It occurs in the wild in the mountainous and moist areas of Europe and Asia. In Poland, the typical subspecies grows in the Sudetes and the Carpathians. In Germany it is known as Kümmellikör, in Poland Alasz.

Allasch, 500 ml:

Caraway infusion*, 125 ml

Star anise infusion**, 15 ml

Lemon skin infusion***, 10 ml

Sugar syrup 73%, 150 ml

Alcohol 75%, 200 ml

1. In a jar, mix infusions with water, then mix with sugar syrup.

2. Keep on mixing and start slowly adding alcohol.

3. Bottle and age for one month.

Notes:

Caraway infusion*: 25 g caraway, 250 ml 50% alcohol, 3 weeks.

Star anise infusion**: 10 g anise, 50 ml 50% alcohol, 3 weeks.

Lemon skins infusion***: 10 g skins, 50 ml 75% alcohol, 3-4 days maceration time.

Amaretto Liqueur, 500 ml

Almond infusion* 100 ml

Vanilla infusion** 15 ml

Brown sugar syrup 73%***, 150 ml

Alcohol 75%, 250 ml

Caramel, 10 ml

1. Mix infusions with alcohol. Add caramel.

2. Pour alcohol into brown sugar syrup.

3. Bottle and age for one month.

Notes:

* 100 g finely crushed almonds, 200 ml 75% alcohol. Macerate for 3 weeks, strain and filter.

** 10 g vanilla stick, 90 ml 50% alcohol. Macerate for 3 weeks, strain and filter.

*** Bring 420 ml of water to about 89° C (176° F). Add 700 g of white sugar and 300 g of brown sugar. Stir until sugar is dissolved. Add 1 g of ascorbic acid, bring solution to a boil and boil for 15 minutes. Keep on stirring and remove any foam from the top. Remove from heat and cool.

Anise Liqueur

Anise Infusion:

Star anise, 20 g,

Alcohol 60%, 100 ml

1. Cover star anise with alcohol and macerate for 3 weeks. Shake the jar twice a week.

2. Strain and bottle.

Anise Liqueur:

Anise infusion, 50 ml

Vanilla infusion*, 10 ml

Sugar syrup 73%, 350 ml

Alcohol 75%, 525 ml

Water to complete 1 liter volume (~75 ml)

1. Mix anise and vanilla infusion with alcohol.

2. Stir sugar syrup and add alcohol.

3. Bottle and age for one month.

Notes:

* vanilla stick, split and cut up, 10 g, alcohol 50%, 90 ml. Macerate for 3 weeks. Strain and bottle.

Extracts such as cloves, cinnamon and almond are also often added.

Banana Chocolate Liqueur

We all know that bananas taste good when covered with chocolate so this should not come as a surprise that a combination of cacao powder and banana infusion creates a wonderful drink, too.

Banana Chocolate Infusion:

Banana, 500 g

Vanilla, 4 g (1 stick)

Alcohol 60%, 500 ml

1. Peel of the skin and slice banana.

2. Place in a jar sliced banana, vanilla and alcohol.

3. Macerate 3 weeks. Shake the jar twice a week. Strain and filter.

Banana Chocolate Liqueur:

Banana infusion 300 ml

Bitter chocolate, 100 g

Sugar syrup 73%, 200 ml

White rum, 100 ml

Alcohol 75%, 300 ml

Orange skins infusion*, 10 ml

1. Break chocolate into small pieces. Mix with rum and 200 ml of 75% alcohol and stir. Leave for a day or two until chocolate is dissolved. Shake the jar from time to time.

2. Add sugar syrup and mix. Add 100 ml of 75% alcohol and stir.

3. Bottle and age for one month.

Notes:

* 10 g orange skins (without pith), 50 ml 75% alcohol, macerate 3 days, strain and bottle.

Strawberries may be added to infusion as they go well with chocolate and banana.

Benedictine Liqueur

Making Benedictine Infusion:

Angelica 10 g

Arnica (flower) 10 g

Cloves 5 g

Cardamom 5 g

Cinnamon 7 g

Ginger 4 g

Hyssop (Hyssopus) 10 g

Lemon balm (Melissa officinalis) 5 g

Lemon skins, dry 12 g

Peppermint (Mentha piperita) 7 g

Nutmeg 6 g

Orange skins, dry 25 g

Saffron 0.25 g

Vanilla 2 g

Wormwood 6 g

1. Mix all ingredients with 750 ml 50% alcohol. Macerate for 2 weeks. Shake every second day.

2. Strain, filter and bottle.

Benedictine Liqueur:

75% alcohol, 500 ml

Sugar syrup 73%, 400 ml

Brandy, 30 ml

Benedictine infusion, 40 ml

1. Take 40 ml Benedictine infusion and mix with alcohol and brandy. Mix with sugar syrup.

2. Bottle and age for 3 months.

Notes: original Benedictine is made by distilling herb/spice infusion.

Cacao Liqueur

Cacao Infusion:

Cacao powder, 50 g

5 g (1 tsp.) freshly ground coffee

Alcohol 50%, 500 ml

Vanilla stick 2 g (1/2 stick) broken into pieces, 3 broken almonds, 1 clove and 1 cm long cinnamon stick.

1. Mix all ingredients with alcohol and macerate for 2 weeks. Shake the jar twice a week.

2. Filter and bottle.

Cacao Liqueur:

Cacao infusion, 350 ml

Orange skins infusion, 30 ml

Citric acid, 0.3 g (3 ml 10% solution)

Sugar syrup 73%, 400 ml

Alcohol 75%, 250 ml

1. Mix cacao infusion with alcohol.

2. Add citric acid to sugar syrup, stir and start adding cacao infusion.

3. Bottle and age for 1 month.

Notes:

* 10 g orange skins, 50 ml 75% alcohol, macerate 3 days, strain and bottle.

Calamus Liqueur

Sweet Flag (*Calamus acorus*) is a wetland weed which has been known for its medicinal and other properties for thousand years. It has been used medicinally for a wide variety of ailments, and its aroma makes calamus essential oil valued in the perfume industry. It is widely employed in modern herbal medicine as its sedative, laxative, diuretic, and carminative properties. In Europe *Acorus calamus* was often added to wine and alcohol infusions. Calamus infusion displays flavor reminiscent of brandy or cognac having the same color.

Calamus Infusion:

Calamus grass, 8 g
Angelica, 5 g
Lemon balm, 5 g
Peppermint, 2 g
Dry orange skins, 3 g
Alcohol 50%, 250 ml

1. Place all ingredients in a jar, cover with alcohol and macerate for 3 weeks. Shake the jar twice a week.
2. Strain and filter.

Calamus Liqueur:

Calamus infusion, 40 ml
Sugar syrup 73%, 400 ml
Citric acid, 0.5 g or 5 ml of 10% solution
Saffron for yellow color if needed, just a touch
Alcohol 75%, 525 ml
Water, as needed to top 1 liter mark (~50 ml)

1. Mix all ingredients. Bottle and age for one month.

Chartreuse

Chartreuse Infusion:

Angelica 12.0 g

Arnica (flower) 2.0 g

Cloves 13.0 g 13 g

Cardamom 1.2 g

Cinnamon 2.6 g

Coriander 12.0 g

Hyssop (Hyssopus) 10.0 g

Lemon balm (Melissa officinalis) 12.0 g

Peppermint (Mentha × piperita) 3.0 g

Nutmeg 2.0 g

Saffron 0.25 g

Star Anise 1.0 g

Wormwood 10.0 g

1. Mix all ingredients with 750 ml 50% alcohol, macerate for 2 weeks, shake every second day.

2. Strain, filter and bottle.

Chartreuse Liqueur:

500 ml 75% alcohol

Sugar syrup 73%, 400 ml

Brandy 30 ml

Chartreuse infusion 40 ml,

1. Mix 40 ml Benedictine infusion with alcohol and brandy. Mix with sugar syrup.

2. Bottle and age for 3 months.

Notes:

Original Chartreuse is made by distilling herb/spice infusion.

Cherry Chocolate Liqueur

** Cacao Infusion:*

Cacao powder, 50 g

5 g (1 tsp.) freshly ground coffee

Alcohol 50%, 500 ml

Vanilla stick 2 g (1/2 stick) broken into pieces, 3 broken almonds, 1 clove and 1 cm long cinnamon stick.

1. Mix all ingredients with alcohol and macerate for 3 weeks. Shake jar twice a week.

2. Strain and filter.

*** Cherry Infusion*

Cherries, 400 g

Alcohol, 70%, 500 ml

Cloves, 2

1. Place cherries in a jar, add cloves and alcohol.

2. Macerate for 3 weeks. Shake jar twice a week.

3. Strain and filter.

Cherry Chocolate Liqueur

Cacao infusion* 200 ml

Cherry infusion** 350 ml

Sugar syrup 73%, 300 ml

Alcohol 75%, 150 ml

1. Mix all ingredients together.

2. Bottle and age one month.

Chocolate-Mint Liqueur

Cacao Infusion:

Cacao powder, 50 g

5 g (1 tsp.) freshly ground coffee

Alcohol 50%, 500 ml

Vanilla stick 2 g (1/2 stick) broken into pieces, 3 broken almonds, 1 clove and 1 cm long cinnamon stick.

1. Mix all ingredients with alcohol and macerate for 3 weeks. Shake the jar twice a week.

2. Filter and bottle.

Mint Infusion:

Peppermint (*Menthae piperitae*), 10 g

Alcohol 50%, 100 ml

Macerate 3 weeks, strain and filter.

Chocolate-Mint Liqueur:

Cacao infusion, 350 ml

Mint infusion, 50 ml

Citric acid, 0.3 g (3 ml 10% solution)

Sugar syrup 73%, 350 ml

Alcohol 75%, 250 ml

1. Mix cacao infusion with alcohol.

2. Add citric acid to sugar syrup, stir and start adding cacao infusion.

Add mint infusion.

3. Bottle and age for 1 month.

Coffee Liqueur

Coffee Infusion:

Ground coffee, 50 g

Alcohol 50%, 500 ml

2 g (1/2 stick) broken into pieces vanilla stick, 3 broken almonds, 1 clove and 1 cm long cinnamon stick.

1. Mix all ingredients with alcohol and macerate for 2 weeks. Shake the jar twice a week.

2. Filter and bottle.

Coffee Liqueur:

Coffee infusion, 350 ml

Lemon skin infusion*, 40 ml

Sugar syrup 73%, 350 ml

Alcohol 75%, 250 ml

1. Mix lemon skin infusion with alcohol, add coffee infusion and mix.

2. Mix infusions with sugar syrup.

3. Bottle and age for 1 month.

Notes:

*10 g lemon skins, 50 ml 75% alcohol, macerate 3 days, strain and bottle.

Coffee-Orange Liqueur

Coffee infusion*, 300 ml

Orange skin infusion** 50 ml

Lemon juice, 15 ml

Sugar syrup 73%, 350 ml

Alcohol 75%, 250 ml

Water, to fill to 1 liter mark (~50 ml)

1. Mix alcohol with orange skin and vanilla infusions. Add coffee infusion.

2. Mix infusions with sugar syrup.

3. Bottle and age for one month.

Notes:

* 50 g freshly ground coffee, 500 ml 50% alcohol. 2 g (1/2 stick) broken into pieces vanilla stick, 3 broken almonds, 1 clove and 1 cm long cinnamon stick.

Mix all ingredients with alcohol and macerate for 2 weeks. Shake the jar twice a week. Filter and bottle.

**20 g lemon skins, 100 ml 75% alcohol, macerate for 3 days, strain and bottle.

Cranberry Ginger Liqueur

1. Cranberry Infusion:

Dry cranberries, 200 g
Alcohol 50%, 1000 ml
Cloves, 2
Cinnamon, 2cm
Nutmeg, ¼ nut

1. Mix everything together with alcohol.
2. Macerate for 3 weeks. Strain and filter. This is your first infusion which you can keep for blending spirits. Cranberry goes well with anything that is sweet such as honey, strawberry or raspberry.

2. Ginger Infusion:

100 g diced ginger
500 ml 70% alcohol
Macerate for 3 weeks. Strain and filter.

3. Lemon Skins Infusion:

10 g lemon skins (without pith)
50 ml 75% alcohol
Macerate for 3 days. Strain.

Cranberry Ginger Liqueur

Cranberry infusion, 300 ml.
Ginger infusion, 100 ml
Sugar syrup, 300 ml
Lemon skins infusion, 30 ml
Alcohol 75%, 250 ml
Water, fill to 1 liter mark

1. Mix all infusions with 75% alcohol.
2. Mix infusions with sugar syrup.
3. Bottle and age one week.

Optional step: Add 200 g of sugar and 500 ml of 40% alcohol to leftover fruit, macerate for 3 weeks. Strain, filter and bottle. This is your second infusion.

Notes:

Dry cranberries are sweetened. Taste infusion for sweetness before adding sugar syrup. Fresh cranberries infusion: 750 g cranberries, 750 ml 50% alcohol. Spices as above.

English Liqueur

The following traditional recipe comes from 1910 Polish classic "Universal Cook Book" (*Uniwersalna Ksiazka Kucharska*) by Marya Ochorowicz-Monatowa.

1. With a fork puncture 4 oranges and 3 lemons, add 1 vanilla stick, 4 cm cinnamon stick, and 3 cloves. Place all in a large glass jar.

2. Cover with 95% alcohol* and macerate for 4 weeks.

3. Discard lemons, cut oranges in half and squeeze out the juice. Add juice to alcohol.

4. Measure the amount of infusion, but keep it separately. For each 1 liter of infusion take 1 kg of sugar and mix with 500 ml of water. Bring sugar syrup to a boil, remove any foam from the top. Take the syrup away from the heat source.

5. Start slowly adding alcohol to the hot syrup, stirring continuously.

6. Let it cool and then filter.

7. Bottle and age for 2 months.

Notes:

*Use 75% alcohol if 95% type is not available.

Goldwasser Liqueur

Goldwasser (in German *Gold water*), was originally made from 1598 - 2009 in Gdansk (in German *Danzig*), Poland. It is 40% herbal liqueur which consists of about 20 herbs and roots. The striking characteristic of the liqueur are the 24 carat gold flakes which are suspended in alcohol. Since 2009 it has been produced in Germany as Danzinger Goldwasser.

Goldwasser Infusion:

Star anise, 5 g
Cinnamon stick, 2 g
Cloves, 2 g
Nutmeg, 3 g
Cardamom, 2 g
Coriander, 4 g
Lemon balm, 4 g
Peppermint, 2 g
Rosemary, 1 g
Dry lemon skins, 6 g
Dry orange skins, 8 g
Alcohol 50%, 500 ml

1. Place all ingredients in a jar, add alcohol and macerate for 3 weeks.

2. Strain, filter and bottle.

Goldwasser Liqueur:

Goldwasser infusion, 40 ml
Brandy, 15 ml
Sugar syrup 73%, 400 ml
Alcohol 75%, 500 ml.

1. Mix infusion, brandy and sugar syrup. Add alcohol.

2. Bottle and age for 2 months.

Kahlua Coffee Liqueur

Kahlua Mexican Coffee Liqueur is the finest coffee liqueur in the world. It is unlikely that it can be replicated at home, however we can try to do our best. Top quality coffee will produce the best result.

Coffee Infusion*, 250

Vanilla Infusion**, 50 ml

Alcohol 75%, 300 ml

Brown sugar syrup 73%, 350 ml

Water, 50 ml

*50 g freshly ground coffee, 500 ml 50% alcohol, 2 g (1/2 stick) broken into pieces vanilla stick, 3 broken almonds, 1 clove and 1 cm long cinnamon stick.

Mix all ingredients with alcohol and macerate for 2 weeks. Shake the jar twice a week. Filter and bottle.

** 10 g vanilla pods, 90 ml 50% alcohol. Macerate for 3 weeks. Strain and bottle.

Kahlua Coffee Liqueur:

1. Mix infusions with alcohol, then mix with brown sugar syrup. Add water to bring the solution to 1 liter mark.

2. Bottle and age for one month.

Notes:

Trying to duplicate famous liqueurs requires some experimenting. Tests can be performed on a smaller scale, for example 100 ml total drink volume.

Kiwi Coffee Liqueur

Kiwi infusion*, 60% 300 ml

Coffee infusion**, 50% 50 ml

Orange skin infusion***, 30 ml

Vanilla extract/infusion ****, 20 ml

Sugar syrup 73%, 350 ml

Alcohol 75%, 250 ml

1. Mix all infusions together.

2. Add sugar syrup.

3. Stir liqueur and add alcohol.

4. Bottle and age for one month.

Notes:

*Kiwi, 500 g, alcohol 70%, 500 ml, 3 weeks.

** Ground coffee, 100 g, 900 ml 50% alcohol, 2 weeks.

***Orange skins, 10 g, alcohol 75%, 50 ml, 4 days.

**** Vanila stick, 10 g, 50% alcohol, 90 ml, 2 weeks

Kumquat Liqueur

Kumquats are the small yellow to orange citrus fruits being approximately the size and shape of an olive with sweet spongy rind and somewhat acid pulp that are used chiefly for preserves, marmalade, and jelly. As the rind is sweet and the juicy center is sour, the raw fruit is usually consumed either whole or only the rind is eaten. Kumquats are popular as a garnish for cocktail beverages, and make wonderful kumquat liqueurs.

Kumquat Infusion:

Kumquats, 500 g

Alcohol 75%, 500 ml

Cloves, 2

Cinnamon stick, 1 cm

Ginger, 5 slices

1. Cut kumquats into halves, remove seeds.

2. Add ginger, cloves, cinnamon and alcohol.

3. Macerate for 3 weeks. Strain and filter.

Kumquat Liqueur:

Kumquat infusion, 400 ml

Sugar syrup 73%, 300 ml

Alcohol 75% 250 ml

Water, 50 ml

1. Mix kumquat infusion with sugar syrup. Add alcohol.

2. Bottle and age for one month.

Loquat Liqueur

The loquat (*Eriobotrya japonica*), is a fruit tree in the family Rosaceae, indigenous to central China. The tree grows in the whole Mediterranean basin and all over Florida. In Mexico it is known as "Nispero." Its nickname is Japanese plum or Chinese plum. Loquat fruits, growing in clusters, are oval, rounded or pear-shaped, 3–5 cm long, with a yellow or orange color. Loquat is eaten as a fresh fruit and mixes well with other fruits in fresh fruit salads or fruit cups. The fruits are also commonly used to make jam, jelly and chutney, and are delicious poached in light syrup. Loquats are also be used to make wine. Lemon or lemon zest is often paired with the wine because the fruit has very low acidity. The fruits are the sweetest when soft and orange. The flavor is a mix of peach, citrus and mild mango.

Loquat Infusion:

Loquats, 750 g
Alcohol 75%, 750 ml
Vanilla stick, 1/2
Cinnamon, 1 stick
Cloves 2,
Ginger, 5 slices

1. Squeeze out the brown seeds. Save 10% of seeds for infusion (uncrushed). Place loquats in a jar, add spices and alcohol.
2. Macerate for 3 weeks. Shake jar twice a week.
3. Strain and filter.

Loquat Liqueur:

Loquat infusion, 400 ml
Lemon skins infusion*, 15 ml
Sugar syrup 73%, 300 ml
Alcohol 75% 250 ml
Water, 50 ml

1. Mix kumquat infusion with sugar syrup. Add alcohol.
2. Bottle and age for one month.

Notes:

*10 g lemon skins, 50 ml 75% alcohol, macerate 3 days, strain and bottle.
Loquat seeds have an aroma reminiscent of bitter almonds (the flavoring of almond extract). Sour cherries pits also exhibit this characteristic. Up to 20% seeds can be added to infusion.

Mandarin Liqueur

The following traditional recipe comes from 1910 Polish classic "Universal Cook Book" (*Uniwersalna Ksiazka Kucharska*) by Marya Ochorowicz-Monatowa.

1. Place in a jar 10 mandarin oranges and 1 vanilla stick (4 g). Cover with 2 liters 95% (or 75%) alcohol.

2. Macerate for 4 days. Squeeze out the juice and strain.

3. Mix 2 kg sugar with 1 liter water and bring to a boil. Remove any foam from the top.

4. Take away from the heat source and pour alcohol infusion into hot sugar syrup, stirring the solution.

5. Filter liqueur and pour into bottles.

6. Age for 3 months.

Orange Liqueur

This infusion calls for an unusual technique that makes an interesting show piece. The taste is slightly bitter due to the orange skins which were macerated for 3 weeks.

Mandarin oranges (2), 300 g

Sugar syrup 73%, 250 ml

Alcohol 75%, 400 ml

Lemon juice, 30 ml (2 Tbsp)

Cloves, 12

Vanilla, 3 g (1 stick)

Cinnamon stick, 2 cm

Whole nutmeg, 1/3

1. Bring water to a boil, switch off the heat and immerse whole oranges for 2-3 minutes.

2. Make 12 short cuts on orange skins all around. Place one clove in each of them.

3. Place oranges and all ingredients except sugar syrup inside a jar.

Add alcohol.

4. Macerate for 3 weeks.

5. Remove oranges, cut and squeeze the juice off. Pour infusion through a strainer. Filter through paper towel.

6. Add sugar syrup. Shake the jar until sugar mixes with infusion.

7. Pour into bottles.

8. Age one month.

Orange-Spice Liqueur

Spice Infusion:

Cinnamon 2.0 g

Cardamom, 1.0 g

Cloves 2.0 g

Coriander 2.0 g

Ginger 10.0 g

Orange skins, dry 20.0 g

Vanilla stick 3.0 g

Place ingredients in a jar, add 200 ml 50% alcohol, macerate for 3 weeks. Strain and bottle.

Orange-Spice Liqueur:

Spice infusion, 50 ml

Sugar syrup 73%, 400 ml,

Rum 30 ml

75% alcohol, 500 ml

1. Mix spice infusion with rum and alcohol.

2. Mix infusion with sugar syrup.

3. Bottle and age for one month.

Persico Liqueur

Crushed almonds, 100 g

Cinnamon, 10 g

Cloves, 3

60% alcohol, 750 ml

Sugar syrup 73%, 400 g

1. Place crushed almonds and spices in a jar and add alcohol.

2. Macerate for 7 days. Strain and filter.

3. Mix with sugar syrup.

4. Bottle and age for one week.

Pineapple Liqueur

Pineapple Infusion:

Pineapple, 500 g

Ginger, 2 slices

Alcohol 70%, 500 ml

Dice pineapple into 1 cm chunks (you can leave the skin on) and cover with 500 ml 75% alcohol. Add ginger slices. Macerate for 3 weeks. Strain and filter. Save the fruit**.

Pineapple Liqueur:

Pineapple infusion, 300 ml

Lemon skins infusion**, 15 ml

Alcohol 75%, 350 ml

Sugar syrup 73%, 350 ml

1. Mix lemon skin infusion with alcohol. Mix pineapple infusion with sugar syrup. Combine both liquids.

2. Mix infusions with sugar syrup.

3. Bottle and age for one month.

Notes:

Pineapple can be fresh or canned.

* 10 g lemon skins, 50 ml 75% alcohol, macerate for 3 weeks, strain and bottle.

** Make the second infusion. Add 250 ml of 40% alcohol and 200 g of sugar to the leftover fruit.

Macerate for 3 weeks. Strain, filter and bottle. You will get sweet

pineapple vodka.

Raspberry - Kiwi Liqueur

Absolutely great liqueur. Raspberry syrup is very sweet and like honey benefits from citric acid. Lemon juice of course could be used, but the solution will become cloudy and impossible to clarify. Kiwi juice tastes great by itself but displays a hint of acidity. Both juices complement each other and create a wonderful liqueur.

Infusions:

Kiwi 500 g, alcohol 60%, 500 ml, 2 cloves. Macerate for 3 weeks. Strain, filter and bottle.

Raspberry 500 g, alcohol 70%, 750 ml. Macerate for 3 weeks. Strain and bottle.

Raspberry-Kiwi Liqueur:

Kiwi infusion, 200 ml,

Raspberry infusion, 250 ml

Sugar syrup 73%, 300 ml

Alcohol 75%, 250 ml

1. Mix infusions together.

2. Mix infusions with sugar syrup.

3. Keep on stirring and add alcohol.

4. Bottle and age one month.

Raspberry Liqueur

Raspberry syrup is very sweet and like honey benefits from citric acid. Lemon juice of course could be used, but it introduces a degree of cloudiness.

Raspberry Infusion:

Raspberry infusion: raspberry 500 g, alcohol 70%, 750 ml. Macerate for 3 weeks. Strain and bottle.

Raspberry Liqueur:

Raspberry infusion, 350 ml

Sugar syrup 73%, 300 ml

Alcohol 75%, 250 ml

Lemon skins infusion*, 20 ml

Citric acid, 0.5 g

Water, to bring liqueur to 1 liter mark (~100 ml)

1. Add citric acid to raspberry infusion and mix with sugar syrup.

2. Mix lemon skin infusion with 75% alcohol.

3. Keep on stirring infusion and start slowly adding alcohol.

4. Bottle and age for one month.

Notes:

* 10 g lemon skins, 50 ml 75% alcohol, macerate for 3 days. Strain and bottle.

Vanilla Liqueur

The following traditional recipe comes from 1910 Polish classic "Universal Cook Book" (*Uniwersalna Ksiazka Kucharska*) by Marya Ochorowicz-Monatowa.

1. Take 30 g of vanilla sticks (about 10) and break them into 2 cm pieces.

2. Cover with 250 ml 95% alcohol* and macerate for 1 week. Strain and filter.

3. Take 2 kg sugar and 1 liter water and bring to a boil. Remove any impurities (the foam) and take away from the heat source.

4. Start slowly adding 1 liter of 95% alcohol* to the hot syrup, stirring continuously. Add vanilla infusion.

5. Let it cool down and bottle.

6. Age for 2 months.

Notes:

*Use 75% alcohol if 95% type is not available.

Crèmes

Crème de Arabica

Coffee Infusion:

50 g freshly ground coffee,

2 g cut up vanilla (1/2 stick), 3 broken raw almonds,

500 ml 50% alcohol

1. Place ingredients in a glass jar, add 500 ml 50% alcohol and macerate for 2 weeks. Shake every 2 days.

2. Strain and filter.

Crème de Arabica:

Coffee infusion, 425 ml

Sugar syrup (73%), 425 ml

75% alcohol, 150 ml

1. Mix coffee infusion with sugar syrup. Add alcohol.

2. Bottle and age for 2 months.

Notes:

You can add Crème de Arabica to any coffee that you drink.

Crème de Butterscotch

Vodka 500 ml

Butterscotch candy, 250 g

Egg yolk, 12 eggs

Sugar 150 g

5 ml vanilla extract OR 20 ml of vanilla infusion*

0.1 ml (4 drops) of sweet orange essential oil OR 20 ml of orange skins infusion**.

1. Place vodka and Butterscotch candies in a jar, cover and shake. Shake periodically until all candy dissolves in vodka.

2. Filter the above infusion through a funnel lined up with paper towel or coffee filter.

3. Place 12 egg yolks in a bowl and add sugar.

4. Mix egg yolks with sugar using electric mixer for 5 minutes until perfectly smooth.

5. Continuing mixing and start slowly adding Butterscotch infusion. Add vanilla and orange flavorings.

6. Mix all together and bottle.

Notes:

* 10 g vanilla, 90 ml 50° alcohol, macerate 3 weeks, strain and bottle.

** 10 g orange skins, 50 ml 75° alcohol, macerate 3 days, strain and bottle.

You may see white foam on top which are air bubbles. They will disappear next day.

Crème de Cacao

Cacao liqueur is a wonderful drink that goes extremely well with cakes and deserts.

Cacao Infusion:

50 g cacao powder,

1 tsp freshly ground coffee, 2 g cut up vanilla (1/2 stick), 4 broken raw almonds,

500 ml 50% alcohol.

1. Place ingredients in a glass jar, add 500 ml 50% alcohol and macerate for 2 weeks. Shake every 2 days.

2. Strain and filter.

Crème de Cacao:

Cacao infusion, 425 ml

Orange skins infusion*, 30 ml

Sugar syrup (73%), 400 ml

75% alcohol, 150 ml

1. Mix cacao infusion with sugar syrup. Mix orange skin infusion with 75% alcohol.

2. Combine infusions together.

3. Bottle and age for 2 months.

Notes:

* 10 g orange skins, 50 ml 75% alcohol, macerate 3 days, strain and bottle.

Crème de Cassis

Crème de cassis is a sweet, dark red liqueur that is made from black currants. A specialty of Burgundy, it is also made in Anjou, Luxembourg and Quebec. Black currants grow in cold climate in the USA,

Canada, Northern Europe and Asia.

Black currants, 300 g

Alcohol 75%, 450 ml

Sugar syrup 73%, 300 ml

1. Crush berries and cover with alcohol.

2. Macerate for 3 weeks.

3. Strain and filter.

4. Add sugar syrup.

5. Bottle and age for one month.

Notes:

Cassis makes a popular cocktail called Kir.

Kir

In a white wine glass add:

2/10 Crème de Cassis

8/10 Chilled dry white wine.

Kir Royal

In a champagne flute add:

2/10 Crème de Cassis

8/10 Champagne

Chocolate Crème

75% alcohol, 200 ml

White rum, 40%, 50 ml

Brandy, 50 ml

Egg yolks, 100 g (6)

Full fat milk, 3.2%, 150 ml

Bitter chocolate, 50 g

400 ml fine sugar, 400 g

Almond infusion*,30 ml

Vanilla infusion**, 15 ml

Orange skin infusion***, 15 ml

Instructions:

1. Break chocolate into smaller pieces and mix with rum, brandy and 200 ml 75% alcohol. Rest for two days, shake often.

2. Separate egg yolks from whites.

3. Mix sugar and egg yolks together. Continue mixing and add liquefied chocolate. Add milk, almond and vanilla infusion.

4. Bottle and age for one month.

Notes:

*25 g almonds, finely crushed, 50 ml alcohol 75%, macerate for 3 weeks. Filter and bottle.

** 10 g vanilla, 90 ml alcohol 50%, macerate for 3 weeks. Filter and bottle.

*** 10 g orange skins (without pith), 50 ml 75% alcohol, macerate 3 days. Strain and bottle.

Egg Crème

250 ml 75% alcohol

30 ml brandy

20 ml rum

200 ml (12 large egg yolks)

400 g fine sugar

30 ml vanilla infusion*

** 5 ml nutmeg infusion

Instructions:

1. Separate egg yolks from whites.

2. Mix sugar with egg yolks until creamy and perfectly smooth.

3. Continue mixing and start adding slowly vanilla infusion, brandy and rum.

4. Continue mixing and start adding slowly 75% alcohol.

5. Bottle and age one month.

Notes:

* 10 g vanilla, 90 ml 50% alcohol, macerate 3 weeks, strain and bottle.

** 10 g nutmeg, 90 ml 50% alcohol, macerate 3 weeks, strain and bottle.

Eggs – 2%, about 12 large eggs (200 g) per 1 l of product. One egg yolk weighs about 17 g.

Storage: 12 months in refrigerator, 6 months at 15° C.

Don't add more than 5 ml (1 tsp.) of nutmeg infusion. Nutmeg can easily overpower other flavors.

Egg Crème with Cream

This crème is similar to a typical egg cream such as Dutch Advocaat or Polish Eiercognac. However it is made with heavy cream and less eggs so its consistency is thinner.

Egg yolks, 150 g (about 9 eggs)

Sugar 300 g

Heavy cream (18%), 200 ml

Alcohol 75%, 350 ml

Almond extract* 15 ml (1 Tbsp)

Cinnamon extract* 5 ml (1 tsp)

Nutmeg extract*, 3 ml (1/2 tsp)

Vanilla extract* 20 ml

1. Mix all extracts/infusions with 75% alcohol.

2. Using electrical or manual mixer mix egg yolks with sugar until creamy and perfectly smooth.

3. Continue mixing and start adding slowly heavy cream.

4. Continue mixing and start adding slowly the mixture of infusions.

5. Pour into bottles and age one month.

Notes:

* Making spice extracts: take 10 g of spice, 90 ml of 50% alcohol, macerate 3 weeks, strain and bottle.

Polish Eiercognac

350 ml 75% alcohol
200 ml (12 large eggs)
400 ml fine sugar
20 ml vanilla infusion*

Instructions:

1. Separate egg yolks from whites.
2. Mix sugar with egg yolks until creamy and perfectly smooth.
3. Continue mixing and add vanilla infusion and alcohol.
4. Bottle and age for one month.

Notes:

* 10 g vanilla, 90 ml 50% alcohol, macerate 3 weeks, strain and bottle.

Vanilla Crème

Vanilla Crème Infusion:

Vanilla stick (6) 20 g
Almonds, finely crushed, 3
Alcohol 70%, 250 ml

1. Mix all ingredients together and macerate for 3 weeks. Filter and bottle.

Vanilla Crème:

Vanilla infusion, 200 ml
Sugar syrup 73%, 450 ml
Brandy or cognac, 50 ml
Alcohol 75%, 300 ml

1. Combine vanilla infusion with alcohol, add brandy/cognac.
2. Mix with sugar syrup.
3. Bottle and age one week.

Useful Information

Medium orange – 220 g

Medium lemon – 150 g

Grapefruit, 400 g

Kiwi – 100 g

Green walnut – 35 g

Egg yolk – 17 g

Sugar, 1 teaspoon – 4 g

Sugar, 1 Tablespoon – 12.5 g

Honey, 1 liter = 1.4 kg

Honey, 1 kg = 0.7 liter

Sugar syrup 73%, 1 liter = 1 kg

(There is 1 kg sugar in 1 liter of syrup)

One US quart = 946.35 milliliters

One US cup = 236.58 milliliters.

One US fluid ounce = 29.57 milliliters

1 ounce = 28.35 g

1 lb. = 453 g

1 kg = 1000 g

1 liter = 1000 ml

1 liter (1000 ml) of water weighs 1 kg (1000 g)

1 ml of water weighs 1 g.

Links of Interest

General Supplies

The Sausage Maker http://www.sausagemaker.com

Allied Kenco Sales http://www.alliedkenco.com

Ebay http://www.ebay.com

Amazon http://www.amazon.com

Wholesale Bulk Foods http://www.bulkfoods.com   grains, herbs, spices, berries.

Candy Warehouse http://www.candywarehouse.com brand candy

Wine and Beer Making Supplies

Homebrew Heaven http://store.homebrewheaven.com distillation and wine, beer making supplies.

Midwest Supplies http://www.midwestsupplies.com homebrewing and winemaking.

Wine Making Superstore http://www.winemakingsuperstore.com wine making supplies, equipment.

Quality Wine & Ale Supply http://www.homebrewit.com wine and beer making supplies.

E.C.Kraus Wine & Beer Supplies https://www.eckraus.com wine and beer making supplies.

Homebrewers http://www.homebrewers.com wine and beer making supplies.

Essential Oils, Berries, Herbs, Plants and Trees

Mountain Rose Herbs http://www.mountainroseherbs.com essential oils, hawthorn, elderberries.

High Winds Herbs http://www.highwindsherbs.com rowan berries.

Haag Farm http://www.walnuts.us green walnuts, walnuts.

Local Harvest http://www.localharvest.org green walnuts.

eGardenSeed http://www.egardenseed.com/   elderberry, herbs, spices.

Edible Landscaping Online http://ediblelandscaping.com cherry dogwood, plants and trees.

Raintree Nursery http://www.raintreenursery.com Plants: Dogwood (Cornus Mas), Hawthorn, Berries.

Forest Farm http://www.forestfarm.com plants and trees, image gallery.

Lincoln Oakes Nurseries http://www.lincolnoakes.com plants and trees.

Making Essential Oils

WikiHow http://www.wikihow.com/Make-Essential-Oils

How to make essential oils http://www.howtomakeessentialoils.net/

Essential-oil-mama.com http://www.essential-oil-mama.com/make-your-own-essential-oil.html

Distillation Equipment

Home Distillation of Alcohol http://homedistiller.org/

Moonshine-Still http://moonshine-still.com/

Smiley's Home Distilling http://www.home-distilling.com/

Hillbilly Stills http://www.hillbillystills.com/

Alembics http://www.alembics.co.nz

Destilarias Eau-de-Vie - Iberian Coppers http://www.copper-alembic.com

Strong Alcohol

Luxco® http://www.luxco.com Everclear® 75% and 95% alcohols.

General

The Alcohol and Tobacco Tax and Trade Bureau (TTB) http://www.ttb.gov/index.shtml regulations.

USA Nutrient database http://ndb.nal.usda.gov detailed data on any product we eat.

USDA Plants Database http://plants.usda.gov/java/profile?symbol=ARVU plants and herbs.

BONAP's North American Plant Atlas http://www.bonap.org a list of plants anywhere within North America

Index

Other Books by Stanley & Adam Marianski

Home Production of Quality Meats And Sausages bridges the gap that exists between highly technical textbooks and the requirements of the typical hobbyist. The book covers topics such as curing and making brines, smoking meats and sausages, making special sausages such as head cheeses, blood and liver sausages, hams, bacon, butts, loins, safety and more...

ISBN: 978-0-9824267-3-9

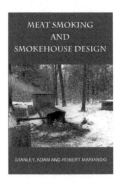

Meat Smoking & Smokehouse Design explains differences between grilling, barbecuing and smoking. There are extensive discussions of curing as well as the particulars about smoking sausages, meat, fish, poultry and wild game.

ISBN: 978-0-9824267-0-8

The Art Of Making Fermented Sausages shows readers how to control meat acidity and removal of moisture, choose proper temperatures for fermenting, smoking and drying, understand and control fermentation process, choose proper starter cultures and make traditional or fast-fermented products, choose proper equipment, and much more...

ISBN: 978-0-9824267-1-5

Polish Sausages contains government recipes that were used by Polish meat plants between 1950-1990. These recipes come from government manuals that were never published before, which are now revealed in great detail.

ISBN: 978-0-9824267-2-2

Sauerkraut, Kimchi, Pickles and Relishes teaches you how to lead a healthier and longer life. Most commercially produced foods are heated and that step eliminates many of the beneficial bacteria, vitamins and nutrients. However, most of the healthiest vegetables can be fermented without thermal processing. The book explains in simple terms the fermentation process, making brine, pickling and canning.

ISBN: 978-0-9836973-2-9

Making Healthy Sausages reinvents traditional sausage making by introducing a completely new way of thinking. The reader will learn how to make a product that is nutritional and healthy, yet delicious to eat. The collection of 80 recipes provides a valuable reference on the structure of reduced fat products.

ISBN: 978-0-9836973-0-5

The Amazing Mullet offers information that has been gathered through time and experience. Successful methods of catching, smoking and cooking fish are covered in great depth and numerous filleting, cleaning, cooking and smoking practices are reviewed thoroughly. In addition to mullet recipes, detailed information on making fish cakes, ceviche, spreads and sauces are also included.

ISBN: 978-0-9824267-8-4

38952327R00156

Made in the USA
Middletown, DE
05 January 2017